EXPLORE
BERLIN

An incomplete list of things, people and developments that passed and/or are passing through
Berlin. Like you and me. A kind of city collage in
chronological-chaotic order.

Patched together by:
Travis Elling

Patching assistant: HollyN

Impressum

© Text und Fotos: Travis Elling

© Coverbild: iStockphoto - Mickis-Fotowelt

© Foto U-Bahn: pexels.com - anna-m. w.

© Reisebuch Verlag 2020

Parkstraße 16

D-24306 Plön

Alle Rechte vorbehalten

Reisebücher in Print und Digital - Reisecontent

www.reisebuch-verlag.de

verlag@reisebuch.de

ISBN: 978-3-947334-37-7

The *Teufelsberg* (devil's mountain) of today was to be replaced by the university complex of the Nazi world capital *Germania*; instead, after the Second World War, the partly built-up area was covered by a large part of the city's ruins and became Berlin's second highest "mountain". From the early 1960s onwards, an iconic US listening station, the *Field Station Berlin*, occupied the very top. After the withdrawal of the *American National Security Agency* in 1991 and a short interim use by the German air surveillance, the mountain and the facility became a paradise for sprayers, mountain bikers, hang-gliders and lovers of ruins. In the 2000s, director David Lynch and the *Maharishi Foundation* wanted to build a peace university with a *Tower of Invincibility* there. That went wrong. By now, professionally guided tours through the old listening station are on offer. Unfortunately, this story is not told here. By the way, the mountain got its name from the neighboring *Teufelssee* (devil's lake). Which, in turn ...

Table of Contents

1933-1945: Berlin-Germania

1945-1989: West-Berlin and East Berlin

1989-?: Berlin unified: Too sexy for itself?

Introduction ...

"Berlin is repulsive, loud, dirty and grey, it's all construction sites and congested streets – but I feel sorry for all who do not live here!"

(Anneliese Bödecker)

Quotes similar to the one above accredited to Mrs. Bödecker are popular all around the world – invariably describing big, desirable cities. However, they are commonly assigned to movie stars, business icons or at least scholars: people who are higher up in the pecking/hipness order of the world. Mrs. Bödecker was reportedly a mere social worker. When and where the quotation saw the light of day is unknown to me, but it somehow fits and aptly expresses a very popular feeling regarding Berlin. Somehow the city is different, although one really can't say why. In 2017, a ZEIT article by authors avowedly fond of living in Berlin declared the metropolis the *"capital of failure"*. The garbage collection system is far from flawless, administration is too slow, supreme expertise in rejecting any and all responsibility for whatever problem may arise is regarded as a fundamental Berlin virtue. Even the dead have to wait for their funeral certificates for weeks. What's so great about all that? *"Here I am Man, here dare it to be"*, as Goethe wrote.

The legendary German poet also quipped: *"Berlin ... is inhabited by such a daring breed of people ... that one needs to have a sharp tongue and be ready to get a bit rough at times."* Goethe, who visited (and survived) Berlin on numerous occasions, must have commanded a pointed lingua.

The idea of this text is to point out which ideas, art movements, people, which developments or historical timelines have passed through or began/ended in Berlin, a city somewhere on the edge of meaning. Clearly, such a text could be written about many or even all major cities of the world. Often, the themes would be identical or similar. After all: one thing all metropolises have in common is their universal attraction.[1] Berlin, like all big, desirable cities, is a cultural-chemical reaction with an uncertain outcome.

Before the Nazis, Berlin had a rather good reputation. The city stood for great advances in science and technology. Industrial history was made in Berlin. The Borsigs supplied the growing rail networks of Prussia and Europe with locomotives and founded a new neighborhood for their factory workers in Borsigwalde. With "Siemensstadt", entrepreneur Wilhelm von Siemens shaped an entire

---

[1] Much worth mentioning was left out: Döblin, the achievements of the Charité hospital, the Edeka supermarket chain, the first cinematic appearance of a disco ball in the film *Berlin: Symphony of a Metropolis ...*

district of Berlin. In the part of central Berlin dubbed *Feuerland* (burning country) or *Birmingham of the Mark*, because of the large concentration of sooty businesses working with metal, only the AEG factory building constructed at the end of the 19th century and some streets named after industrialists (Borsigstr., Pflugstr., Schwartzkopffstr. etc.) remind us of Berlin's past as a place shaped by officially commemorated industrialists and completely forgotten workers. Berlin is considered one of the birthplaces of the computer, which has such a defining impact on today's world. At the same time, the birthplaces of discoveries are ... often somewhat indefinable. Most important inventions are based on the preparatory work of others elsewhere, after all, and they also often happen more or less simultaneously in different locations. The localized origin of revolutionary ideas is thus mostly rather anecdotal, a mere question of detail.

0-1700:

Pre-history, the Middle Ages and the Berlin of the Electors

[Sculpture of the bull of the Goddess Hel by Paul Mersmann, Alboinplatz, Schöneberg-Tempelhof]

#Schildhorndenkmal, Blanke Helle

To begin at the beginning...

– Big bang; it's just possible that just about anything is possible. First matter is formed; somewhere, there is a piece of something that somehow someday becomes sun, earth, Brandenburg, that island in the Spree ... Unity and order become diversity and disorder ... Neanderthals wonder what life is all about, the very occasional Roman tourist takes notes ... Berlin's prehistory begins.

The area bordering the rivers Havel and Spree is first mentioned around 100 AD by the Roman Tacitus in his *De origine in situ Germanium Liber*. According to him, the Semnones lived here until they started to feel a certain longing for the southern sun, emigrated, merged into the Alamanni and became part of the Suebi/Swabians[2], who, according to Tacitus, were, like all pre-migration Germans, tall, red-haired and (at least the males) pretty lazy and addicted to alcohol whenever away from the battlefield. They also offered human sacrifices on occasion and tied their hair in a so-called *Suebenknoten* (Suebian knot[3]).

---

[2] "Schwabe" is a rather vague term (it basically means people talking in that funny Swabian dialect of southwest Germany). It is not my intention to establish a more than anecdotal connection between the Semnones, or some other group alive several centuries ago, and modern-day people.

[3] Such a knot was actually found on a preserved bog body: the Osterby Man.

Even if Tacitus' geographical details seem rather vague, German prehistory scholars have identified the Semnones as the original Berliners. Modern Berliners appear to still have some historical gut feeling about the early presence of the Semnones/Suebians in this area; perhaps there is some unspoken concern about them reclaiming Berlin as their rightful tribal, ancestral, promised land? After most of those early would-be-Berliners emigrated to the warmer south around the year 400, a variety of Slavic clans settled in the vacated area. Their larger settlements included Copnic (Köpenick) and Spandau. In the middle of the 12th century, according to the official version, Christianizing Germanic tribesmen from the West pushed East. Then, Albrecht the Bear (an Askanian and part of the Swabian aristocracy from Schwabengau) fought against the Slavic prince Jacza or Jaxa de Copnic. Legend has it that Jaxa escaped from the bearish Teuton and found himself close to drowning, helplessly pulled to and fro by the mighty Havel near Spandau. Desperate, he begged the Christian God for help, and presently was washed upon a small peninsula. A man of his word, Jaxa is said to have converted on the spot; he hung up his shield and horn on the next tree, and thus gave the place his name: Schildhorn (shield-horn). The story is regarded as the founding myth of the Mark Brandenburg; and a myth it likely is. Today it is assumed that Jaxa, like many other Slavic rulers, was born a Christian.[4]

[4] The *Spandauer Kreuz*, an object that seems almost Celtic in style (at least to my layman's eyes) is said to have served in a church in Slavic Spandau shortly before the year 1000. A re-cast of the cross is on display in the Neues Museum.

The Schildhorn monument, erected in 1845 on the assumed site of the aforementioned salvation and Christianization of Jaxa of Köpenick, is a suitable place for commemorating Berlin's early history. The design is by the Prussian architect Friedrich August Stüler, although Friedrich Wilhelm IV had given him rather concrete royal ideas regarding what shape would be acceptable. It is not particularly pretty.

There is another interesting story dealing with the Christianization of the Berlin area, which raises further questions. Ancient legends have it that the entrance to hell itself used to be located near what is now the Alboinplatz in Schöneberg. It is said that, in pre-Christian times, a priest made sacrifices to Hel here, the Germanic goddess of the underworld and mistress over Helheim (Hel's home = the Germanic hell). For his services, Hel had a black bull rise from the depths of the murky pool, to aid the holy pagan in the cultivation of the surrounding fields. At some point, a Christian monk took over field and sanctuary, but, putting his trust in the Christian God above, he no longer sacrificed to Hel. Fuming as only German goddesses fume, she sent her black bull up again – not to help farm the land, but to drag the impertinent monk into the depths of hell (or, in another version, to devour him). So ... Christianization failed? Really?

Legends and folk stories rarely come with dates of origin, meaning that we are left wondering about when that story was supposed to have happened, and who told it. It is considered a part of the Germanic-pagan mythological cosmos and therefore should hail from the time before the departure of the old Semnones. Alfred the Bear supposedly spearheaded a host of Christian settlers, after all, who superimposed themselves on a Slavic population (note: the "devil" of the old Slavs was called Veles, and is considered a protector of cattle). Perhaps the Slavic Berliners liked to tell some good old stories they had heard from the old Germanic (non-Christian) inhabitants around the fireplace in the evenings, or some Semnone had remained in the "old homeland", eking out a living as a storyteller. Perhaps the whole thing was just somehow superimposed on the ethnic-religious situation, or even moved from Slavic to the Germanic mythology at a later time?

Hel's Pfuhl is commemorated today by a rather monumental sculpture of the murderous bull, erected in 1934, which, of course, has an interesting history. It was created as part of a Nazi support program for unemployed (Aryan) artists. The regime did not appreciate the artwork of sculptor Paul Mersmann, however, and even wanted to remove it. A modern legend has it that Mersmann, an upright German artist with little taste for the Nazis but who needed the money, filled the stomach of the bull with anti-fascist flyers. One wonders: is this true, or just another legend meant to help modern Germans to cope with the difficult past of their country? Hel's Pfuhl is definitely a good place to consider the pitfalls of the past and the common need to rewrite history.

[A part of the Nikolaiviertel, regarded as Berlin's old town; the neighbourhood, almost completely destroyed in World War II, was rebuilt as a new old town starting in 1982 and completed for the 750th anniversary celebrations in 1987.]

*Nikolaiviertel

Cölln is mentioned; and becomes Berlin

The (Christian) towns of Cölln, located on an island in the Spree, and Berlin, established on the banks of the river and set halfway between Spandau and Köpenick, were first mentioned shortly after Brandenburg was taken over by Alfred the "bear" of the Holy Roman Empire of the German Nation. More precisely, a contract dated October 28, 1237 concerning the payment of the tithe (church tax) mentions a certain *Symeon, parish priest of Cöln* – meaning the place must somehow have existed. Berlin, basically a few houses scattered around the Nikolaikirche, was first mentioned in 1244. Soon afterwards, the first Berlin (city) wall was documented, and Cölln erected a *Gerichtslaube* (a medieval court house) close to the former town hall. Directly next to it they kept a pillory and a gallows handy, i. e. at a conveniently short distance. Much later, in 1871, the structure was removed and rebuilt in the Babelsberg Park, where it still stands today. It is not an urban surrounding. If you visit the *Laube*, you just need to do a little mental photoshopping to replace the few visible buildings scattered among the woodlands with actual greenery and feel transported to a time before the massive explosion of mankind.

In the historicizing *Nikolaiviertel*, generally considered the old town of Berlin, but now mainly a hotchpotch of prefab buildings and some reconstructed structures without much life of its own except for being a tourist attraction, a copy of the building was erected for Berlin's 750th anniversary celebrations in 1987. Here, the restaurant *Zur Gerichtslaube* offers what are called authentic Berlin dishes.

Speaking of authentic Berliners: some sources say that the people who first settled in the area in the course of the Germanic Christianization moved from the Rhineland (hence the name "Cölln"?) and today's Holland into "*uncharted territory*". In 1307 the two towns merged to form the twin city of Berlin-Cölln. The remains of the first Berlin Wall, up to six meters high and designed to protect the city against human predators roaming the unsafe Brandenburg expanse, can be found on Waisenstraße. In the plague years 1348/49, the still young city lost a good part of its inhabitants – not only because of the plague.

Soon after the plague started to take its toll, some "respectable" citizens blamed the Jewish community. Persecutions, expulsions and pogroms took place – in Berlin, and in many other places in Central Europe. In 1446 Elector Friedrich II ordered Jewish believers to leave the Mark Brandenburg. But by 1510, Jews were again suffering in Berlin. At that time Jews from Brandenburg were brought to the city and then sentenced to death at the stake. The claim? Host desecration. Torture led to confessions. Another horribly common occurrence in central Europe at that time. A memorial stone behind the residential house Mollstraße 11 in Berlin-Mitte, between Moll– and Berolinastraße, commemorates this cruel history. The plaque on the stone was placed in a nearby synagogue in 1935, which no longer exists. The memorial stone was erected in 1988. Unfortunately, Berlin's early days do not speak to us of alternative ideas or a tolerant lifestyle, but of the standard cruelty of humanity.

1417

Oh! Those (not so) indomitable Berliners!

When the ruling dynasty of the Ascanians ran out of male descendants around the end of the 14th century, the Mark Brandenburg and Berlin-Cölln went to the Wittelsbach family, who sold the area 50 years later. What? Yes, Berlin was squarely sold to the highest bidder. OK, it wasn't all that simple. The then Brandenburg elector Otto V Der Faule (The Lazy) had to accept the transfer of the Mark Brandenburg to the dynasty of the Luxembourgers against the payment of 500,000 guilders according to the iron will of the Roman-German Emperor Charles IV, who was then residing in Prague. As a result, the city of Tangermünde (in Saxony-Anhalt) was expanded into a residence and had a good stab at playing an important role in the future of the region. But as early as 1417, the Mark was transferred again, this time to Friedrich VI, a Hohenzoller, by Sigismund of Luxembourg (a son of Charles IV and later a Roman-German emperor). Sigismund needed cash to pay for increasing military expenditures elsewhere.

Following the transfer, Burgrave Friedrich IV (of Nuremberg) became Friedrich I (of Brandenburg) and the first Elector of the Mark. He demoted once proud Tangermünde and made Berlin-Cölln his (twin) city of residence. But like many other cities, Berlin-Cölln strove for at least a quantum of independence from the ruling powerful lords with their armies of mercenaries. An independence that did not find much favour in the eyes of the upper crust.

Berlin-Cölln had even joined the Hanseatic League and, at the height of their impudence, dared to erect a *Roland*[5]. When Elector Friedrich II *Eisenzahn* (Iron Tooth) wanted to present Berlin-Cölln with a palace for him to live in, the citizens smelled oppression. In 1448 the *Berliner Unwille* (Berlin Resistance) broke out: an open rebellion against *Eisenzahn* and his palace. The Berliners could not compete with his knights, however, and the hapless Roland was – according to legend – drowned in the Spree. In addition, Berlin's miffed ruler forbade the city from ever again becoming a member of the Hanseatic League, something Eisenzahn thought was detrimental to the peace of his benign reign over Brandenburg. Instead, the palace was built. Surprisingly, although by no means successful the *Berliner Unwille* became an often cited indication of Berlin's "ungovernability", a popular myth history does not really support. Like

---

[5] Rolands are statues of the legendary knight Roland/Hruotland, common in today's northern and eastern Germany, intended to remind people of the history told in the old French Song of Roland. They symbolize freedom and resilience. Today's best-known Roland stands in Bremen, where an archbishop is said to have burned the first (wooden) Roland of the rebellious city to cool their jets. In Bremen the anti-Roland-brutalities had no success; a new statue was built in 1404, this time made of stone.

any utopia projecting diagonally into reality, Berlin's identity is mainly wishful thinking.

Yet in 1905 Berlin got another Roland – this time a copy of Brandenburg's Roland, which today guards the entrance to the *Märkisches Museum*. A suitable place to think about civil liberties and the arrogance of the mighty. The museum is within easy walking distance from the (at the time of writing: almost) rebuilt Stadtschloss (city palace). At least in my memory, the reconstruction or partial reconstruction of the structure blown up after the war inspired little love among the citizens – especially, it seems, among those who did not sit on expert committees. Many wished for an architectural inclusion of the Palace of the Republic (the East German parliament), demolished for this purpose, as a reminder of the history of the GDR. But the democratic experts and private pro-castle sponsors had different ideas. Berlin, they argued, needs its palace back! And maybe justly so, as there was no real new *Berliner Unwille* against its construction. More like a grumbling, soon silenced by the pro-castle media hype.[6]

---

[6] The castle Hohenzollern, ancestral seat of the eponymous family, deteriorated in the 18th century as a result of various military occupations. The Prussian King Friedrich Wilhelm IV had the castle restored in the mid-19th century, showing enthusiasm for his family history – an early anticipation of Berlin's "re-castleization"? The work was carried out by leading Berlin architect Andreas Schlüter, the Burggarten was created by Peter Lenné, famous for his Berlin parks. Later, some usable remains of the Kaiser Wilhelm Memorial Church destroyed in WWII were brought to the castle down south.

[The Borussia statue in the Preußen-park, Charlottenburg-Wilmersdorf.]

Berlin gets to be Prussia's beating heart

From 1230 onwards, the Teutonic Order conquered the lands east of Branden-burg, where the wild and very pagan Pruzzen roamed, with the approval of the Polish Prince Konrad of Mazovia, who had his problems with those non-too-docile barbar-ians (they were no match for the Teutonic Order, though).[7] In the resulting monastic state, the indig-enous (whatever that word means) inhabitants of the region mixed with the Slavic and Germanic Christians who were moving into the now pacified areas, until the Pruzzen of Protoprussia were only just detectable in homeopathic doses. When the Teutonic

---

[7] The prince is said to have consulted the Teutonic Order, his brothers in faith, in matters concerning his rowdy neighbors, but historians are not certain about the details, and some believe the Teutons falsified history somewhere down the line. The relevant first treaty between Conrad of Mazovia and the representatives of the order was lost; subsequent treaties drawn up by the then Pope have survived, however.

State broke up during the Thirteen Years' War, two new countries emerged: "Royal Prussia", which was under the protection of the Polish crown, and the hereditary Duchy of Prussia, headed by Albert, Duke of Prussia. This second state became Protestant (and boasted the world's first protestant state church). It later fell, in the course of the marital politics common at the time, into the hands of the rulers of Brandenburg, and from 1618 onwards the Berlin Hohenzollern ruled over Brandenburg-Prussia. In the course of the subsequent Thirty Years' War they often sought protection in the eastern part of their now sprawling empire from turmoil elsewhere. At some point, the term "Prussia" was applied to the entire Berlin Empire, if you want to call it that.

Back in the days of rampant national pride, Prussia was personified by the goddess Borussia; today, there is a replica of a corresponding statue in the *Preußenpark* (Prussian Park) near Fehrbelliner Platz.[8] As the text on the pedestal of the statue informs us it was a gift presented to the city of Berlin by the German State in 1936. The Preußenpark is now usually referred to as *Thaipark* (Thai park); in summer, Thais living in Berlin, their German relatives and other city dwellers come together in an atmosphere reminiscent of a giant picnic.

---

[8] Berlin was likewise personified in the 19th century – by the Berolina. Several statues were fashioned of this lady, who was possibly considered the most beautiful Berliner until Nefertiti came to the city in 1924, including one on Alexanderplatz. All that remains of that particular Berolina is the name of the neighboring building; the statue was melted down in 1942 for munitions.

1671

Uncle Friedrich Wilhelm wants you!

The term *Prussian tolerance* usually refers to the admission of refugee groups after the Thirty Years' War (1618-1648), which claimed the lives of so many people that it became necessary to "refresh" the local population, and to the French Protestants taken in under the Potsdam Edict of 1685. As early as 1671, however, some Jewish families expelled from Vienna were invited to settle in Brandenburg/Berlin – against payment of a "protection tariff" collected by the aristocratic mafia. Unfortunately, they would indeed need protection. In 1573, the last Jewish community of Brandenburg-Berlin was (again) expelled after vicious pogroms–likely to have been partially fueled by some of Luther's at times strongly anti-Semitic statements. But a good 100 years later everything seemed … different. The rulers hoped that the new tolerance would stimulate the weak economy. Originally, however, these new Berliners were not allowed to build synagogues–that would have been a little bit too much for Berlin's otherwise tolerant Christians.

The first Synagogue, on Heidereutergasse in today's Mitte district, was only inaugurated in 1714. It became the *Old Synagogue* following the inauguration of the

New Synagogue on Oranienburgerstraße in 1866. For the building of the *Old Synagogue*, the ingenious architect lowered the ground a little; the structure was not allowed to be higher than the surrounding buildings, but needed to be tall enough inside to incorporate a so-called "women's gallery", since, according to tradition, the genders had to be separated during religious services.

The new, massive synagogue of 1866, on the other hand, was allowed to cast its splendor proudly across the Berlin skyline. The *Old Synagogue* was destroyed in 1945 during an Allied air raid. Today, only the foundation walls next to a memorial plaque can be noted, directly behind a monument for the *Rosenstraße Miracle*.[9] It is an interesting, but also ... somewhat unsightly place.

In 1685, the Edict of Potsdam invited Huguenots fleeing France to settle around Potsdam. Friedrich Wilhelm and the upper classes hollered a hearty *"bienvenue"* to

---

[9] The *Rosenstraße Miracle* happened in 1943, when the Nazis wanted to deport the last remaining Berlin Jews and gathered them in a building on Rosenstraße. Many of them were married to (in Nazi terms) "Aryan" women in "mixed marriages" and were tolerated (although begetting children was forbidden). Many of the wives and other relatives of the detainees showed courage and gathered in the street, where they demanded the release of the men. And ... it worked. Was it just a postponement granted by the Nazis to pacify the population momentarily, or did the women permanently save their husbands? Who knows. However, this story raises the question what might have been possible in those dark times with a little more civic courage than the individual German Aryan tended to show.

the new Berliners, while the lower classes slowly mixed with them and exchanged recipes. Incidentally, these were not the first French Protestants in Berlin. Since religious tolerance in France had for some time offered a somewhat sorry picture, whoever identified as Protestant simply left if possible, i.e. if they had the money. Rich people mostly preferred the more expensive but much more advanced London. But in 1685, Friedrich Wilhelm needed workers – simple people who would build a new life for themselves and enhance his city. For this he promised a temporary exemption from tax payments, plus civil rights and cheap or even free land. The offer was widely accepted; in 1700, a good 20% of the Berlin population consisted of French refugees. The Huguenots lost their special status only in 1809 – in the course of the Prussian reforms after the withdrawal of the Napoleonic occupying power.

A good place to remember the history of the Huguenots is the former Lindenmarkt, today's *Gendarmenmarkt*, which was built in 1688. Many of the newly arrived Huguenots settled in the area, and around 1700 a French and a German church were erected there as a symbol of peaceful coexistence. The former, now called the "French Cathedral" – the original church plus an added tower – also houses the *Huguenot Museum*.

1700-1871:

Berlin, home of the Prussian kings

[A bridge in the Charlottenburg palace garden, one of the few baroque gardens in Germany.]

1701

A King is born – in Königsberg

On January 18, 1701, Brandenburg's Margrave Friedrich III crowned himself "King Friedrich I in Prussia" in Königsberg, the capital of the Dutchy of Prussia. Although the potentate had to pay the Holy Roman emperor, the clergy and other interested parties handsomely to be allowed to raise his rank, he thought the investment worth it. An important point: Friedrich I would be the royal sovereign of an area outside the Holy Roman Empire – Prussia. Berlin was "inside", and as king in Prussia (and not in the Holy Roman Empire), he could act more freely, as he would not be directly subordinate to the emperor. This also helps to explain why Prussia eventually became the name for the entire kingdom of the Berlin rulers. Friedrich III/I also made it clear that he would do things his way by crowning himself. It was an act of clear symbolism: He subordinated himself only to God, not to the clergy, the self-proclaimed representatives of the assumed super-power in the Hereafter.[10] A side note: although both he and his wife Sophie-Charlotte, crowned by him, were anointed by Protestant bishops, the pope never recognized the Prussian king.

A decisive factor for the approval of the then Emperor of the Holy Roman Empire, Leopold I (residing in Vienna at the time),

---

[10] He may have been inspired by the Swedish King Charles XII, who made news in Europe in 1697 with his symbolic self-coronation as lord over the then giant Swedish empire.

was probably the death of Carlos II in 1700, with whom the Habsburgs' reign in Spain was to end, as he had somehow bequeathed his throne to a French Bourbon. That did not sit well with Leopold I, a Habsburg. With the coming War of the Spanish Succession in mind, he would have wanted to make Friedrich I, King in Prussia, a military alley of the Habsburgs, or at least not an enemy. Friedrich I managed to keep his dominion largely out of the international bloodbaths of his time.

Friedrich I, later often portrayed as weak, since he was not particularly belligerent, and sometimes called *Schiefer* Fritz (Lopsided Fritz) because of a crippled shoulder, also laid the foundation for entities that would later become important for Berlin and Prussia. In 1696 he founded the *Academy of Painting and Building*, which became the *Prussian Academy of Arts*, and in 1700 the *Scientific Society of the Margrave of Brandenburg*, later the *Royal-Prussian Academy of Sciences*. In his free time he frequently indulged in pomp and circumstance; he had the *Bernsteinzimmer* (Amber Room) made for his Berlin City Palace, and built a summer residence for his second wife Sophie-Charlotte in the nearby village of Lützow. After her death, the *Lützenburg* (Castle Lützen) was renamed to *Charlottenburg* (Charlotte's Castle) and spawned a city.

After Friedrich I's death in 1713 his son Friedrich Wilhelm I, the soldier king, made it his mission to cleanse Berlin of all the luxuries and the pomp his father had cluttered the city with, among them the *Bernsteinzimmer*. Hard work and military matters were more his thing.

Berlin Blue

Pigments have been used as colorants since prehistory, but for a long time people depended on the narrow gamut of naturally occurring substances. When Spain's conquistadors explored Latin America, they found new dyes that meant a minor revolution (and more color) for European art and fashion. The next big color thing followed in around 1704, when a chemist working in Berlin discovered, by chance, the first modern synthetic pigment. The deed is attributed to Johann Jacob Diesbach, who had moved to Berlin from Switzerland and worked in the laboratory of the famous alchemist Johann Konrad Dippel. Dippel was looking for a way to produce artificial gold, as alchemists do, and is considered a possible (but not certain) inspiration for the "scientist" Frankenstein from Mary Shelly's eponymous fantasy novel.

This first modern synthetic pigment is today called *Berlin Blue*, or *Prussian Blue*. Also known for its medicinal benefits it is on the WHO's list of essential medicines; Berlin Blue binds heavy metals in the body, such as radioactive cesium, which can enter the environment and people's bodies e.g. after accidents in nuclear power plants. In modern Berlin, a small company utilizes the synthetic pigment to produce a drug called Radiogardase, used to prevent the resorption of some radioactive elements.[11]

As a reminder of the discovery of the first modern synthetic pigment, a visit to the picture gallery of *Sanssouci* Palace is recommended. Here you can find Pieter van der Werff's painting *The Burial of Christ* from 1709. The Dutchman's work is the first known painting to have used the new dye. Another well-known painting that owes its effect partly to the healing pigment is Vincent van Gogh's *Starry Night*, which can be contemplated in New York's Museum of Modern Art.

British engineer Joseph Whitworth, one of the fathers of mass production, found another use for *Berlin Blue* in around 1830; by applying an oily *Berlin Blue* solution (*Engineer's Blue*), he was able to determine the flatness of a workpiece to improve it, if necessary. The process is still used today in tool manufacturing.

[11] Literature has its own producer of *Berlin Blue*; the father of Jenny Treibel in Theodore Fontane's *Frau Jenny Treibel* runs a factory producing the dye.

1734

An Irishman in the Soldier King's Court

Friedrich Wilhelm I (FW I), also known as the "Soldier King", continued the good work of the Prussian Friedrichs: the resettlement of Brandenburg or *repeuplierung* (re-population), as it was then called. In 1732 he welcomed almost 20,000 Protestant refugees from Salzburg at Zehlendorf's village church. The group had fled from the fervently catholic Salzburg bishopry, which back then belonged to Bavaria, a region of the Holy Roman Empire of the German Nation (Salzburg became part of the Austrian Empire in 1816). The refugees were now to be settled in East Prussia.

FW I was also responsible for a rather idiosyncratic subgroup of *Urberliner* (original Berliners): the *Lange Kerle* (Tall Lads). Even as a young prince, the prospective potentate celebrated his lifelong passion for towering men, who, for his taste, needed to stand over six Prussian feet (1.88 m) tall. Such fine specimens, he thought, were worth a lot of money and should be paid well for their tallness – he likely thought of them as some think of supermodels today. He ran a special task force advertising the advantages of being tall in Berlin, such as high wages and sometimes even a piece of land to retire on. Needless to say, "tall lads" from all over the world flocked to the rather small (ca. 1.62 m) Prussian king. He was particularly pleased when James Kirkland from Ireland arrived in Berlin (or in Potsdam, where the regiment was stationed) in 1734. Standing 2.17 m tall he certainly was a rather strapping lad.

To aid in their effect, the *Lange Kerls* wore special grenadiers' caps that towered nearly another half a meter into the Prussian sky above them. Kirkland and his immensely tall colleagues were, by the way, not intended for war time use; they were basically show pieces. This was not true for smaller individuals among the 3,000 soldiers in Friedrich's tall regiment. Anyway, many of them stayed in Berlin, adding to the city's gene pool. Kirkland, for example, became a successful Berlin merchant after the dissolution of the regiment (following the death of FW I in 1740) and died in 1779 in his new home. During Kirkland's lifetime, members of the military and their direct families made up almost 20% of the Berlin population; in 1747, Berlin was home to a military population (active soldiers, their wives and children, and disabled soldiers living on army stipends) of roughly 22,000 people. The total population of Berlin amounted to about 108,000 people that year.

---

[12] The history of the *Bernsteinzimmer* (Amber Room) is also linked to the *Lange Kerls*. The father of FW I, Friedrich I, had the *Bernsteinzimmer* built into his Berlin city palace. Since star architect Andreas Schlüter had already been commissioned to upgrade the palace, it seemed practical to have him design a state room at the same time; voilà, a Prussian marvel was born. But FW I had little love for such pomp; and when Russia's Peter the Great raved about the room during a courtesy visit, FW I offered him a deal: a room in return for soldiers ... tall soldiers. Big guys. Thus, the *Bernsteinzimmer* came to Russia and to St. Petersburg, where it was dismantled by the German army in 1941 and brought to Königsberg. At the end of the war the *Bernsteinzimmer* went missing; in the meantime, however, a copy has been fashioned so that astonished tourists can once again admire the „*8th Wonder of the World*" in the Catherine Palace outside St. Petersburg.

#Böhmisch-Rixdorf/Neukölln/ Richardplatz

Protestants of the world ...
Come to Neukölln!

Richardsdorp, in 1737 just a small village outside Berlin, is another place in Brandenburg marked by refugee immigration; in this case it was Bohemian Protestants fleeing the sometimes brutal re-Catholicization sweeping through their homeland. Friedrich Wilhelm I invited them to settle in this idyllic spot on the road to Berlin and granted them autonomous administrative rights. He went so far as to divide Richardsdorp into Bohemian and German parts (the two municipalities were merged again in 1874 under the name Rixdorf). The town grew to over 200,000 inhabitants, making it one of the larger cities in Germany in 1900. Rixdorf was back then considered more fun than Berlin, as the Schieber (something like German Tango – well, that might be a touch exaggerated; still, it was a dance with lots of body contact and dubious morals) was omnipresent. For the concerned members of higher Berlin society, gently obsessed with traditional values, it all went too far. In 1912 the Schieber was banned, and the city renamed. Neukölln was born; the powers that be might have thought that name sounded a bit more traditional and acceptable. Although the rebranding was not popular with the populace, it stuck.

There are still some old buildings and structures around Richardplatz that reveal its past as a village center. And naturally, by now the *Bohemian village* is regarded more a refuge for wealthy, albeit (or nowadays: for this very reason) hip residents than a place to shake a leg with shady intentions.

Berlin, home of all things "Anti"

Some stories seem to be eternally recurring templates, narrative building blocks of history. Take Plato's futile attempt to persuade the tyrant Dionysius II of Syracuse to establish a secular utopia. The relationship between Voltaire and the Prussian ruler Friedrich II ("the Great") is slightly similar. It all began with an exchange of letters between the young Friedrich and the already famous French philosopher, during which the future Prussian ruler criticized the treatise Il Principe ("The Prince") by the Italian philosopher Machiavelli; the young upstart and idealist Friedrich vowed to defend *"humanity against this monster"*.

Machiavelli's work was at the time broadly considered a handbook for unscrupulous power mongers, so Friedrich's criticism did not so much stem from an ingenious, enlightened, utopian surge of princely inspiration, but rather corresponded to the consensus of the educated classes. Nevertheless, Voltaire was taken by the ideas Friedrich II expressed with youthful verve and encouraged him to write a longer text on the theme. Voltaire probably hoped that the young aristocrat could positively influence his peers. Thus, the *Anti-Machiavelli* was born – in French. It was meant to be a kind of pamphlet against power-hungry princes, or Friedrich II's handbook for good governance.[13] However, by the time Voltaire published the essay in the Netherlands in 1740, Friedrich II had ascended to monarch due to the sudden death of his father and (likely assuming that people would now hold him to certain statements in his work, written in youthful zeal) concealed his authorship. He also stopped the publication of his work in Prussia; in the rest of Europe, Friedrich II's text was read with interest.

In one of those charming historic twists, to be "anti" would be rather en vogue in the later West-Berlin; basically everyone was anti-establishment, anti-Nazi, anti-square, anti-standard and hopefully "antigenic" (alternatively attractive); anti-Machiavelli, of course, too. Still, in the reunited, new and now even hipper Berlin, the band Bonaparte (named after a Machiavelli fan ...) brought this development to its textual peak with their song *Anti Anti*. Or was the whole "anti"-thing always just a tribute to Friedrich II?

Voltaire accepted an invitation by Friedrich II to Sanssouci in 1750. He stayed three years, in which some of his famed works appeared, but the relationship with his

---

[13] Some think that Friedrich II was simply venting his hatred for his father, Friedrich Wilhelm I. When he and an "*intimate friend*" tried to escape his fate as Prussian heir to power, FW I imprisoned his son and his friend in the fortress of Küstrin (the ruins of which are now located directly behind the border to Poland and are well worth the trip). Friedrich II then had to witness his friend's beheading.

royal friend cooled noticeably. Or rather, it heated up. The publication of Voltaire's *Histoire du Docteur Akakia et du Natif de St Malo*, a satire referencing the President of the Prussian Academy of Sciences, is said to have angered Friedrich II so much that he had copies of the book publicly burned on the Gendarmenmarkt, causing the separation of the unequal twosome. However, they eventually forgot the dispute and resumed their correspondence. Nevertheless … perhaps Voltaire meant Friedrich II when he wrote: "*There is always a German at the root of any problem*".

"A moment of happiness is worth more than thousands of years of fame."

(Friedrich II)

Let us endeavor a swift excursion into the practice of judging aristocrats in old Prussia … the *Brockhaus Bilder-Conversations-Lexikon* of 1838 described the ruler as follows: "*Frederick II, the Great and Only, King of Prussia, 1740-86, the founder of Prussia's reputation as one of the great powers of Europe, the wisest and most powerful general in the war, the wisest and fairest Prince in Peace, a friend and connoisseur of the sciences and arts …*" and so on; the *Anti-Machiavelli* was not mentioned in the article.

One nation under one vegetable

When Francisco López de Gómara described the potato in his *Historia General de las Indias* (Gómara worked as a chronicler for the Spanish Conquistador Cortez, but was never himself in the "Indias", or Americas), he sounded a little like a modern apologist for new superfoods. The inhabitants of the new world, Gómara reported, fed mainly on maize and potatoes and usually lived to be "*a hundred and even more years old*". Clearly, the success of the potato in hip Europe, and even in backwards Prussia, was to be enormous. In 1649, for example, one could admire the potato blossom in Berlin's Lustgarten, then a kind of botanical garden. Wait a minute, potato … blossoms? Correct; the potato was first appreciated in Prussia and elsewhere for its "graceful" blossoms.

Friedrich II first became interested in the "superfood" around 1750 (by then, Western Europe and the southern German-speaking countries were already ahead regarding the potato revolution). Having heard of the high nutritional value of the easy-to-grow potato, the enlightened ruler thought: what's not to like? However, the Prussian farmers did not receive the new crop too warmly, despite free seed handouts. Friedrich II had to resort to the ultimate weapon of the absolute ruler and issued a series of so-called "potato orders", the implementation of which he had monitored. He also issued explanations regarding the cultivation and the preparation of the potato; boiled potatoes with salt were recommended for poorer subjects. In his memoirs, the adventurer Joachim Christian Nettelbeck describes the process of the potatofication of Prussia as follows: "*They now showed the assembled crowd the new fruit that had never before been seen by a human eye. In addition, an unintelligible instruction was read out on how these potatoes were to be planted and cultivated, as well as how they were to be cooked and prepared. Of course, it would have been better if a written instruction had been included. For amidst all the turmoil, very few paid attention to the lecture. Then, the good people took the highly praised tubers in their hands, smelled, tasted and licked them, shook their heads and offered them one to the other; they broke them open and even threw them to the present dogs, who tossed them around and also scorned them. (…) 'These things' – they said – 'do not smell and do not taste, and not even the dogs want to eat them. What good would they do us?'*"

By now, Frederick II's endeavors to popularize the potato are the stuff of legends. He is said to have tried to persuade his unwilling subjects by staging raids on his own potato fields in order to get the thick Prussian peasants to understand: These things are valuable! Worth stealing! He is also said to have commissioned pictures of pretty peasant women serving potato dishes, but I was unable to verify this pioneering sex-sells-campaign. Well, it might just be a Prussian legend. Robert Warthmüller's well-known painting *Der König überall* (The omnipresent king), in which Friedrich II inspects the implementation of his potato order, was not painted until 1886, but is a good starting point for reflecting on the history of the potato. It is on display in the German Historical Museum.

> *„Luther shook Germany – but Francis Drake calmed it down again: He gave us the potato."*
>
> *(Heinrich Heine)*

The success of Friedrich II's potato initiatives was, for whatever reason, absolute, as was the triumph of the potato in other parts of Europe. By the middle of the 19th century, the potato had replaced grain as the most important food for ordinary people. When, around 1842, potato mildew found its way from America to Europe on mysterious routes and led to bad if not completely failed potato harvests, the effect was devastating. The great famine of Ireland (*Gorta Mór* in Irish) is well known. There, the potato had fed a massive population explosion since the middle of the 17th century. When it went lacking, the effects were murderous.

The Prussian variant of the potato crisis is less known. After a failed harvest in 1846/47 the Berlin city administration asked Friedrich Wilhelm IV for support, including the suppression of the processing of potatoes into spirits (a kind of vodka was made of potatoes). As elsewhere, the ruling powers saw no reason to give up their profits – or to change the status quo even a bit. Eat cake, guys & gals! Accordingly, the potato prices rose, as did the grumbling among Berlin's customers – the city had just turned into an industrial hotspot with its typical host of poor inhabitants. When ordinary Berliners could hardly afford potatoes – or any other food – anymore, they began to plunder market stalls and shops on the *Gendarmenmarkt* and other markets. To avoid further unpleasantness, the market on *Alexanderplatz*[14] was cancelled completely. Then, a stone flew through one of the windows of the Crown Prince's Palace. The *Potato Revolution* had begun, but was soon quashed again by the ever-effective Prussian army. Nevertheless, it is regarded as a kind of forerunner of the March Revolution of 1848.

[14] Which had been renamed from *Königs Thor Platz* (King's Gate Square) in 1805 on the occasion of a visit by Tsar Alexander I.

Cuddling up to my Kachelofen

[A Kachelofen (tiled stove); now unused, but not unloved.]

One often gets the impression that the concept of *sustainability* has arisen from the modern age and its flagrant consumer excesses. We believe that our distant and not even that distant ancestors were living a sustainable life since they simply lacked the modern stuff needed for overexploitation, right? It might come as a bit of a surprise, but the excessive consumption of natural resources is not that recent a phenomenon. The 18th century, for example, saw dire wood shortages in many areas of Europe.

Georg Carl von Carlowitz, a native of Saxony, noticed this problem on his travels through England (where he was briefly suspected of being a foreign agent responsible for the Great Fire of London) and France, where he considered the modern forest laws of that country with awe. In 1713 he wrote his *Sylvicultura oeconimica*, in which he formulated the concept of sustainability. In 1764 Friedrich II issued an edict ordering his subjects in no uncertain terms never to forget their responsibilities to posterity and the state, and thus to use resources sparingly. At the same time, he tendered a competition for a new wood-saving stove with reduced wood consumption. The winner was a certain Johann Paul Bauer, whose *Berliner Kachelofen* (Berlin tiled stove) included an adjustable air supply as well as other useful elements. It soon became the standard in Berlin and the surrounding area. But alas, this did not save the nearby forests. They were cleared in record time, but as a result the wood needed for heating and industry soon had to be imported at a high cost. A heavy burden for the emerging industrial hotspot Berlin.

Always willing to go for the cheaper option, Berlin's industry kept on relying on other resources, including wind and water power as well as the strength of people and animals to drive the so-called *Göpel*, a kind of horse mill. Then, unsustainable coal found its way into the hearts of forward-looking industrialists and other people in need of a convenient energy source, and Berlin's wood-saving stoves were replaced by coal stoves. These remained typical of Berlin until the end of the 20th century; even around 1990, in winter you could still smell a distinctive note of coal in the air in many a neighborhood in both West- and East Berlin. Apartments with coal heating continue to exist (there is even talk of a new trend). After all, the relationship between Berliners and their tiled stoves has always been good or even intimate (today, there are voices praising the superior, *"more human"* warmth of the tiled stove). A text by the German comedian Joachim Ringelnatz may serve as proof: *"I love you so much! I would give you a tile out of my oven without any hesitation."*

Sustainability itself has become one of the more important modern concepts; in 2015 the United Nations adopted a declaration detailing "Sustainable Development Goals". To commemorate the tiled stove, and to reconsider the goals of sustainability in comfortable warmth, just encourage friends who live with an old tiled stove to have you over for dinner. Or visit the *Museum of Stoves and Ceramics* in Velten, located not far from Berlin and in existence since 1905, housed in one of the factories in which tiled stoves were formerly produced for the Berlin market.

[St-Hedwigs-Cathedral, Bebelplatz, Mitte.]

#St.-Hedwigs-Kathedrale, House of One

The "House of One"–First try

In addition to Protestants fleeing religious persecution, quite a few Catholics seeking work came to
Berlin, especially from Silesia. But their faith presented a problem to Prussia, which liked to pat itself on
its stately shoulder for being a place of uncommon

religious tolerance. There were hardly any Catholic churches left in Berlin. Friedrich II had a rather practical idea: near today's Bebelplatz, a new church for all religious societies was to be built, following the model of the Roman Pantheon, a temple consecrated to all gods. Charles Jordan, then a close confidante of Friedrich II, is said to have dissuaded him from this foolish, utopian idea: *"Catholics"*, he argued, *"should have their own church"*, best named after the patron saint of Silesia, Hedwig von Andechs, as groups of different faiths would never get along in close quarters. The form of the pantheon, however, could be retained, why not? In 1773, *St. Hedwig's Church*, financed by Catholic crowdfunding, was opened – as the first new Catholic church in Berlin after the Reformation. In 1930, it was declared the cathedral of the archbishopric of Berlin. The cathedral is currently being redone, the previously slightly asymmetrical design spreading over two partially open floors is being abandoned in favour of a simple circular shape with a central cult site. Some regret the vanishing of one of the most unusual church rooms in Berlin, others are pleased that the *"empty centre"*, which gave the cathedral its unique character, will finally disappear, giving peace to the more culturally-architecturally conservative members of Berlin's catholic flock. The church superiors themselves write that they are pleased that after the reconstruction, *Normalzentralität* (standard centrality) will be restored.

Currently the *House of One* is being built not far from *St. Hedwig's*, on the former site of the historic Petrikirche, destroyed during the Second World War. The structure is to serve as a prayer house for Christians, Jews and Muslims (and also other faiths? Spaghetti Monster, anyone?). It is not without reason that the initiators of the House of One point out that "*great success, breakdowns and immeasurable guilt are inscribed in Berlin's history*". They'd certainly prefer to be part of one of Berlin's success stories. Fine with me. But perhaps a simple conversion of *St. Hedwig's Cathedral* to *Hedwig's General Reflection Site*, in accordance with the old idea of the Father of Prussia, would have sufficed.

1780

Musika marschierta um die Welta

Friedrich II, Prussia's ruler supreme, is widely considered an exceptional person, among other things because of his high opinion of the arts and his uncanny musical talents. However, the long-held widespread assumption that he composed the Spanish national anthem, originally a military march with the title *Marcha de Granaderos*, and presented the piece to Charles III of Spain as a gift, is but a myth – with an interesting story attached to it: Charles III, so the legend goes, sent one of his military advisers to the court of the Prussian King to study the latest Prussian military tactics. On this occasion, Friedrich II is said to have presented the interested visitor with a short composition, meant to improve marching discipline. One can just imagine Prussia's army, gladly goose-stepping along to the sounds of Friedrich II's flute playing... While a visit with a view to checking out the military secrets of the Prussians seems plausible, the probable author of the Spanish national anthem was a certain Manuel de Espinosa de los Monteros, in the 18th century a professional musician in the service of the Spanish rulers.

At least in Germany, anthems seem to be entities with foreign roots; the Prussian folk anthem *Heil dir im Siegerkranz* (Hail thee who wears the laurel wreath), which later became the imperial anthem, used the melody of *God Save the Queen/King*, originally meant for English potentates and of uncertain authorship. The text was a recycled poem originally addressed to the Danish king. The later German national anthem was based on the melody of the Austrian imperial anthem written by Joseph Haydn; Haydn's probable inspiration was a Croatian folk song.

> *"I don't think there's anything in the world you couldn't learn in Berlin – except the German language."*
>
> *(Mark Twain)*

From the potato to flute concerts – Friedrich II shaped Prussian culture like hardly anyone else. As an enlightened thinker and reformer, he also considered the problems of the German language, which he clearly recognized and described in French; his ultimate point of reference and desire, like that of practically all German-speaking rulers of his time, was powerful, lofty Versailles.

His *Über die deutsche Literatur; Die Mängel, die man ihr vorwerfen kann, die Ursachen derselben und die Mittel sie zu verbessern* (On German literature; its shortcomings and how to overcome them) from 1780 addresses the problems of the lingo of his lamentably non-French-speaking subjects, in his words a *"semi-barbaric tongue that breaks down into as many dialects as Germany has provinces"*. He actively sought reasons for the precarious state of Germanic culture and language, found them in the difficult history of the German-speaking countries – war and conflicts everywhere – and gave a short outline of a suitable teaching program. This was to turn those stubborn Germans into the most cultivated citizens of a beautiful new age, just as once the court of Louis XIV, in the opinion of the Prussian ruler, had lifted France and the formerly crude French plebs from belching barbarism into the refined heaven of culture ... The text resonates with a benign tendency for a "revolution from above" and calls for potentates and scholars to *"challenge and foster"* the base populace: *"Hard-working children should receive small awards, negligent ones soft reprimands."* At the same time, Friedrich II also dealt with the aesthetic problems of the brutish German language: *"It will be difficult to soften the hard sounds which most of our words use. Vowels flatter the ear. Too many consonants in a row hurt it, because they are difficult to pronounce and lack melody. Furthermore, we use many verbs and auxiliary verbs whose last syllable is mute and unpleasant, among them 'sagen', 'geben', 'nehmen'. Add an 'a' to these endings and form 'sagena', 'gebena', 'nimma': such sounds then please every ear."*

Whether one regrets or welcomes it, his latter proposal did not meet with success; Friedrich II clearly did not pursue this project as persistently as the introduction of the "Tartuffel" or potato, see above. He was in any case widely criticized for his literary views within the German scholarly world – in which, as Friedrich II explained in his text, freedom of opinion prevailed.[15] The monarch had likely not read too many contemporary

German-language texts and authors. In its basic tone, however, the often criticized text of the monarch, not a real fan of the German language, is at least constructive – just as an old-fashioned father, so to speak, who tries to take care of the formation of a child perceived by its caring father as somewhat dull and not too promising. Anyway, Friedrich II predicted a flourishing future for German culture and language, easily achieved by implementing his proposals. He ended his text with the assumption that he, Friedrich II, resembled Moses; he can see the promised land (of German culture) but, unfortunately, will never reach it. Strangely, he might even have inhabited the cultured country he so desired – his times saw the creation of some of the great classics of German literature and music – but he was half-blind on one language.

Culture and literature are abundant in the numerous libraries of Berlin. The most interesting is of course the *Staatsbibliothek* zu Berlin near Potsdamer Platz. The building, also called *Bücherkreuzer* (Book Cruiser), is known to a wider audience due to its appearance in Wim Wender's film *Der Himmel über Berlin* (Wings of Desire) and is considered by some, including myself, to be one of the most beautiful and "Berlin-like" buildings of the city.

[15] When Friedrich II spoke of the "*scholarly world*", he likely meant thinkers appointed by him. In the year the text was published, 1780, he issued an order that made "*unauthorized writing*" punishable; among other things, erring writers could be ordered to serve in the army–"*small praise and easy reprimands*", huh?

#Quadriga, Brandenburger Tor

The Quadriga goes a-traveling

In 1806 relations deteriorated between Prussia and the emperor of post-revolutionary France, Napoleon; the French potentate seized the opportunity and conquered what was to be conquered, including Berlin. The Prussian capital surrendered without a fight–which comes as no surprise, given the resounding military successes of the French army on its way towards the East. A few days later the keys to the city where handed to the victorious commander, while the Prussian rulers, aristocrats and generals fled to Königsberg, or to somewhere else in the vast Prussian East. *Der Telegraph*, one of Berlin's early newspapers, wrote on October 27, 1806: "*The entry took place with an order and calmness revealing the real character of the victors (...) The excellent attitude of the French troops, their martial appearance, their decency, their friendliness and cheerfulness were generally admired*".

The French also brought innovations with them – for example some degree of self-government by the citizenry, something pre-Napoleonic Berlin had sadly lacked. Many Berliners fostered sympathies for the occupying forces and the political changes they brought. But Napoleon committed a faux pas; he had the Quadriga removed from the Brandenburg Gate, only completed in 1793, and brought to Paris, where he wanted to have it exhibited on a triumphal arch, as a sign of his victory. The gate was left with a naked iron spike sticking out of it – a sore reminder that the Berliners had allowed themselves be conquered. In 1808, the French troops ended their stint Berlin after the *Peace of Tilsit*. It became clear that the city had only been conquered as a bargaining chip anyway. Berlin was "*restituted*", along with some of the former "*possessions*" of the Prussian king, whereby Berlin per se was only mentioned as part of Brandenburg. The agreement was bitter for the Prussian rulers, whose empire was practically cut in half. A complete dissolution is said to have been prevented only by the influence of Russia. Furthermore, there were reparation payments, enormous debts accumulated by feeding the French troops and other expenses, and even worse – the Quadriga was not returned either. Napoleon wanted to keep her as a victory trophy. One might think this surprise visit had gone a tad too sour, but there was also a good side to it. Berlin's citizens had tasted modern times during the occupation, and they wanted more. In 1810, the first Berlin university was founded by, amongst others, Wilhelm von Humboldt. A (small) step away from the feudal system, which, of course, remained strong in Prussia.

Starting in 1813, the conflict between France and Great Britain, which had been almost global since the end of the French Revolution, turned into a European war of liberation[16] – the suppressed European countries no longer wanted to

[16] The devil is in the details; liberal forces called the conflict in the German-speaking world a "*war of freedom*", since they hoped for a liberal state based on liberal ideas instead of the ultimately family-based aristocratic rule; the "*restoration*" won, however, and through the "*liberation*" of the realm from Napoleon's supreme power wanted to restore things to the former status quo. "*Cobbler, stick to your last*" was a likely motto of the noble families and their court of libertines, artists and soldiers.

submit to the utopian but Franco-centric dictates of Napoleon's monolithic state, which duly collapsed. He basically failed in his attempt to swallow Russia, but the Prussian army was not uninvolved in the battles against the *"ruler of Europe"*. Field Marshal Blücher, also called *General Vorwärts* (General Onwards), was instrumental in the reclaiming of the Quadriga in 1814. The sculpture was then brought back to Berlin, where she assumed her former place on June 30. On her way, she was celebrated in suitable style.

The Quadriga is said to have been received by a cheering crowd in Düsseldorf, where she crossed the Rhine. Once in Berlin, the statue was thoroughly restored and slightly altered according to a design by Schinkel; it now included an iron cross with the date "1813" on it, in memory of the victory over the former occupying forces. The Berliners, always good for a quip, are said to have been so pleased by the return of the pretty ensemble of figures that they dubbed it *Retourkutsche* (tit-for-tat carriage), still a popular term for "getting even". At the same time, the square formerly known as the *Quarre* (rectangle) was given its modern name: Pariser Platz.[17]

---

[17] The Pariser Platz/Rectangle was originally built to complement two other squares, the *Oktogon* (today's Leipziger Platz) and the *Rondell* (today's Mehringplatz), in the 18th century during the redesign of the Friedrichstadt, then a Berlin suburb, at the hands of Philipp Gerlach, who had a soft spot for geometry.

1812

There's a Light, and it never ...

Not every discoverer immediately grasps what it is he or she is discovering; when Galileo Galilei observed an apparently motionless spot in the endless black void of the universe through his telescope in 1612, he assumed it to be a fixed star, but science historians believe he was the first human being to glimpse the distant planet of Neptune. But it was still a long way to the official discovery of Neptune, which began with Wilhelm Herschel, a native of Hanover, who emigrated to England to earn a living as a musician. The talented Herschel devoted himself intensively to music theory and from there found his way to mathematics, which eventually led him to astronomy; in 1781, he discovered a previously unknown planet that he called, in an obvious attempt to flatter the British monarch, *Georgium Situm*, or *George's Star*. Its orbit was then closely observed, calculated and eyed with critical frowns. In 1812, the French scientist Alexis Bouvard published corresponding calculations and suspected another planet behind *George's Star* due to irregularities in its orbit. Urban Le Verrier, in Paris, calculated the expected location of this even more distant planet and then asked Johann Friedrich Galle at the Berlin Observatory to search for an elusive, tiny speck in the dark – after he had received refusals from various other institutions, due to his less-than traditional approach to planet finding. But when Galle checked the calculated location, he found – nothing. Only the meticulous comparison of his observations in the immediate vicinity of the predicted location with existing star maps finally brought success: a new planet had been found, the knowledge of our solar system had increased. But now, a very earthly dispute arose over the naming of those two tiny twinkling lights. *George's Star* and *Herschel* were on offer for the nearer planet, *Le Verrier's Planet, Oceanus* or *Leverrier* were possible monikers for the more distant one. In 1846, the *Academy of Sciences of St. Petersburg* agreed pragmatically to stick to mythological names when naming planets. Thus, the two specks in the dark were given the names Uranus and Neptune, under which we still know them today.

The discovery of Neptune is, of course, essentially based on the efforts of Le Verrier, but the collaboration with the Berlin Observatory is a fine early example of early international scientific collaboration. Le Verrier's method for the discovery of Neptune later also provided decisive evidence for the localization of the dwarf planet Pluto. Unfortunately, the building of the old Berlin observatory is no longer in existence; it was located just above Halle'sches Tor, more or less opposite the present Jewish Museum. Some say the enthusiasm for local co-discovery of Neptune was the decisive factor for the creation of the world's first public observatory, the Urania. Alexander von Humboldt's *Kosmos* lectures are also often cited as an inspiration for the institution. Held from 1827 onwards, his lectures were not aimed at specialists and the "better society", but at the broad Berlin population. Humboldt did not believe that being interested in new things was a quality of the elites, but, simply and quite democratically, of people in general.

The original buildings of the Volkssternwarte are unfortunately no longer preserved. To remember Berlin's connection with the discovery of the stars, visits to the successor of the *Urania*, the *Wilhelm Foerster Observatory*, which has existed on the Trümmerberg Insulaner since 1961, and the modern *Urania*, a lecture, exhibition and event facility in Berlin-Schöneberg, are suitable.

#Monbijou-Park

Faust: Almost a preview

Friedrich II did not have the chance to assess Goethe's famous works, but the latter's *Faust* felt quite comfortable in Berlin. In 1819, at least one version of the work, set to music by the Polish-Prussian Prince Anton Radziwill, premiered in the later German capital – in the since demolished *Monbijou Palace*[18] once situated opposite today's *Bode Museum*. Faust was performed as a chamber music parlor-room happening, so to speak. Radziwill, a native of Vilnius, had found his way to Berlin through his love for the niece of Friedrich II, Luise Friederike. His utopian vision was to build a new Polish-Prussian kingdom; while working for his multicultural vision, he found time to devote himself successfully to music, his second love. The *Faust* living-room performance was repeated several times and was well-received; it even used some cool multimedia elements, more precisely a *laterna magica*-projection of the dramatist's head floating around the walls. The actual premiere of the complete play took place ten years later at the Hoftheater in Braunschweig.

[18] Monbijou was even then mostly a museum; *"patriotic antiquities"* were exhibited there, later it became the *Hohenzollern Museum*. After severe damage during WWII, the palace/museum was demolished in 1959; the name lives on in the *Monbijoupark*.

Industrialize! Industrialize!

Industrialization in the early 19ᵗʰ century saw a sharp increase in Berlin's population, and not only because of the rampant bureaucratic expansion of the city (in 1861, the towns of Moabit, Wedding and Gesundbrunnen were incorporated into Berlin proper). Many workers and people seeking a better life came to Berlin – mostly from Prussian and German-speaking regions and especially from Silesia, which Austria was forced to cede to Prussia in 1842. In 1900, almost 20% of Berlin's industrial workers were born in Silesia.

In his memoirs, the writer Gustav Freytag, a Silesian who studied in Berlin, paints a vivid and not always positive picture of Berlin around 1836: "*We Silesians speak in comfortable, broad tones, while Berliners energetically used their mouths to the full possible extent when speaking, and at times, when they want to show their superiority, they even speak through their noses; we are casual and peaceful in our dealings and tolerate peculiarities in the language and behavior of others with good-hearted courtesy, while Berliners mock everything they think clumsy and ridiculous, always give sharp retorts and rejoice in attacking others. When the people come out of the pubs in the late evenings* in Silesia, we are often noisy, and when groups meet, there's usually plenty of swearing and teasing, after which everyone goes home peacefully. In Berlin, they get straight down to fisticuffs, and every evening we heard from our rooms – we lived on Hackescher Markt – the harsh noises of brawls."

[One of the sculptures in the *Skulpturengarten gegen Krieg und Gewalt* (Sculpture Garden against War and Violence) at the former location of the *Krolloper* (Kroll Opera House)]

#Former site of Krolloper, Reichstag

Kroll's opera

The history of the *Krolloper* begins with a visit by the Prussian King Friedrich Wilhelm IV to Breslau/Wroclaw, then capital of the Prussian province of Silesia. There, made welcome in Joseph Kroll's winter garden, the potentate was swept off his feet by the richly decorated rooms. *"Ro-man-tastic!"* the sensitive king thought, *"I need something like that in Berlin!"* – and asked Kroll to move to Berlin with utmost, irresistible, kingly courtesy. Once there, he was offered a somewhat semi-attractive former parade ground not far from the Brandenburg Gate, which the contemporary vernacular of Berlin is said to have called the Wüste (desert); Kroll still accepted. In 1844, Kroll opened his establishment. Soon, the upper crust congregated there for masked balls and "*Chinese Nights*", enjoying the modern gas lighting and even a brief stint of waltz celebrity Johann Strauß. But after just a little while, the management felt compelled to try to appeal to a broader audience. It was a big house, after all, and it needed to be full to make a buck. But … the luck of the Krolloper was a fickle mistress. In the 1920s, the establishment, no longer under family management, became the *Staatsoper am Platz der Republik* (state opera) and then finally closed in 1931.

"*So what?*", one might ask. The downfall of an institution serving the amusement of those with sufficient cash is certainly not of historical interest. True. If it hadn't been for the Reichstag fire in 1933. The Nazis, who thought of the Reichstag, a symbol of German democracy, as a thorn in their side decided to let it fall into decay and instead met at the *Krolloper* – practically across the street. There, they passed the infamous Enabling Act on March 23, 1933. The Nazi dictatorship had officially begun. The Nazis later used the *Krolloper* for several further meetings; in addition, the first television broadcast in Germany took place here in 1934. So yes, there is a bid of a story there.

After the war, the building continued to be used for concerts and dances until it finally closed its doors in 1956; the building was demolished in 1957. The former location is today a green area between the *Reichstag* and the *Haus der Kulturen*, partly covered with trees and artworks. A perfect place at any time of the year to reflect on what can become of an aristocrat's romantic proclivities. And also one of the few places of (possible) remembrance where one can still feel traces of history without being helped along by curated guidelines. No swank or impressively designed building, no museum explains the historic and cultural meaning of the place where the Nazis declared war. And the works of artists from Europe, Japan, and Israel that were set up here in 1961 are not only abstract, but also almost forgotten. Different. Real. Because no chic building, no explanatory museum "helps" people to understand the meaning in the place where the Nazis declared war. The sculptures seem to have grown, as the grass has grown here, in protest against history. Some will find that this does not do justice to the significance of the place. But, to my mind, it seems to do just that. Because here, people are left alone with a traceable, but almost unexplained past.

#Friedhof der Märzgefallenen

The European revolution fails; in Berlin and elsewhere

[Statue of the "red" sailor at the *Friedhof der Märzgefallenen*.]

Napoleon swept through Europe in the name of his empire, which had grown out of the French Revolution, his efforts at enlightenment by foreign force leaving not only a somewhat stale aftertaste, but also a desire for reforms and more freedom among the general population. Europe's aristocratic clans, meanwhile, tended to prefer a rapid return to the old order. After all – look what happens when simple dabblers try to do the work of professional rulers. Europe had been smoldering practically since the end of the Napoleonic era; in addition, various famines and crop failures had shaken the status quo, among them Berlin's *potato revolution* of 1847. In March 1848, following the February Revolution in France, the Mannheim People's Assembly formulated the so-called *Märzforderungen* (March demands). These were discussed practically everywhere in the German-speaking world. There was fighting on the barricades in Berlin on March 18, 1848, with demonstrators demanding freedom of speech, the right to vote and a constitution. The violence claimed over 200 lives. Despite the none-too-civil behavior of his army, King Friedrich Wilhelm IV tried to stylize himself as the man to restore peace and order, and paid his last respects to the killed revolutionaries on *Gendarmenmarkt*, wearing a black-red-gold sash. These were the colors of the democratic movement. The king wanted to show himself as a partner of the people and promised that Prussia would merge into "Germany", thereby asserting the ideals of the Frankfurt National Assembly.

The people believed him, but His Majesty had other plans and confided to his brother that he had worn the colors of the democratic revolution only to calm the masses. Any reforms already made were taken back; although common suffrage (for all male citizens) was demanded and partly introduced in various German regions in 1848, the counterrevolution, spearheaded by a young Otto von Bismarck, had different ideas. A three-class electoral system was introduced in Prussia in 1849; votes were weighted according to relative tax burden. Ironically, even this seemingly antiquated voting right, far below the aspirations of the national assembly, was one of the most progressive in Europe at the time.

Originally, the victims on both sides of the March barricades were to be buried together – in an attempt to declare the almost-revolution a tragic fratricidal dispute within the Berlin community. But that didn't happen either. The civilian (or rebellious) victims of the fighting were finally laid to rest in a special cemetery – the *Friedhof der Märzgefallenen* (cemetery of the March Victims/Martyrs), located in today's *Volkspark Friedrichshain*. Fallen soldiers were buried in the *Invalidenfriedhof* (cemetery of the invalids), a military cemetery near the Berlin-Spandau canal in walking distance from Berlin's central train station. The *Friedhof der Märzgefallenen* became a symbol of the German democracy movement; the exhibition there is therefore called, perhaps somewhat exaggeratedly, Am *Grundstein der Demokratie* (At the Foundation of Democracy). In 1918, the socialist victims of the November Revolution were also buried here, and the cemetery received its statue of the "Red Sailor" (pictured).

By the way: despite the ancient-looking name plate, the *Platz des 18. März* (March 18th Square) on the western side of the Brandenburg Gate was given its name in the year 2000 (previously it was called *Square in front of the Brandenburg Gate*, and *Hindenburgplatz* during the Nazi period). The name was intended to recall both the revolution of 1848 and the first free elections to the East German parliament on March 18, 1990. The latter saw the newly founded *Alliance for Germany* triumph with 48% of the vote, using the slogan "*Nie wieder Sozialismus*" (Never again socialism) and a clear "*Yes, immediately*" to German reunification. It was, so to speak, an eastern referendum on reunification; in West Germany the constitution and Helmut Kohl were in peaceful consent that no vote was needed.

1851 #Berliner Kindergärten

No games, please, we're Prussian

When the reformer Friedrich Fröbel published his work Die *Menschenerziehung* (Raising human beings) in 1826, he did his part in the revolution in the treatment of children (and let's not forget: Johann Oberlin and Louise Scheppler in Strasbourg and Robert Owen in New Lanark, Scotland had already followed similar leanings). Instead of keeping young people quiet and locked away in child detention centers, they should be allowed to behave according to their age – and not have to comply with the adults' need for peace and quiet, instead being allowed to cavort around in one of Fröbel's kindergartens.

The world's first kindergarten was established in 1840 by Fröbel in Bad Blankenburg (Thuringia). Did the idea then move triumphantly to Berlin (where free kindergarten spots have been a hotly debated topic in recent decades)? Not quite, as the Prussian government did not consider Fröbel's efforts advisable and, in 1851, even banned the establishment of kindergartens altogether because of their *"atheistic leanings"*. Obviously, Berlin was still far from being the *"capital of atheists"* (as the city is today somewhat optimistically called by some, albeit mainly because of its communist past). The ideas of Fröbel and others, who wanted children to grow up *"like plants in a garden"*, were simply alien to the average Prussian official.

Fortunately for the Berlin children, Bertha von Marenholtz-Bülow raged hard against the ban; the aristocrat succeeded in 1860, and Fröbel's dubious institutions were approved – even in Prussia. But perhaps the Berlin authorities simply liked the separation of children according to their ancestry, into offspring of the higher and lower classes, which Marenholtz-Bülow demanded (and Fröbel rejected). In the *Volkskindergärten* (kindergarten for common people) she suggested, the children of the poor should be prepared for their lives as workers through exercises in dexterity and discipline. As Marenholtz-Bülow claimed, children brought up in this way *"would not be ashamed of any work ..., would not shy away from even the lowest efforts, for the good of the whole ... and would not feel their own dignity violated ... because it is done out of love for the common good"*. Ah, yes. The beloved common good of the rich and famous.

Today, there are no Marenholtz-Bülow kindergartens in existence (Fröbel, on the other hand, is a frequent kindergarten name, even if the term itself bears little meaning). But one suspects some still wish for the more gifted and blessed little ones (offspring of more gifted and blessed parents, of course) to be raised in "elite" kindergartens, learning five languages, ten instruments and the art of government, while others get prepped to happily supply for the common good.

"Education must strive to empower,
not to inculcate."

(Friedrich Fröbel)

Prussia gets a German bank

On March 10, 1870, the Prussian crown approved the founding statute of a new bank, the *Deutsche Bank* (DB, German Bank). Until 1870 the German currency was a minor player on the international stage, and most transactions leaving the German Confederation had to be handled via well-established financial institutions in Britain and France, which meant additional costs. The new financial institution, initiated by Adelbert Delbrück and Ludwig Bamberger, was to facilitate trade relations between the German states and the world. But the founding committee also clarified that, to some degree, the impetus of the founding had a "national" angle. The DB was to further the German unification process and to "*secure Germany an appropriate position*" in the financial world.[19] Prussia's high and mighty approved. Naturally, the seat of the Deutsche Bank was to be Berlin, which also was, to

[19] Some consider the DB to be a kind of German National Bank because of its name. This is not so. At the time the company was founded, Prussia's central bank was the Preußische Bank, which became the Reichsbank in 1875. Its former seat, the *Haus am Werderschen Markt*, is one of the largest buildings in Berlin. Built during the Nazi dictatorship, it served as the seat of the Central Committee of the East German communist party from 1959 to 1990. Since 1999 it has been part of the headquarters of Germany's Ministry of Foreign Affairs.

the Prussian centralist mindset, the destined capital of the future Germany. But for all the city's later might, choosing Berlin as the site of the headquarters was, at first, an act of a mostly symbolic nature, as the international business connections of the Prussian capital lagged behind those of the North German Hanseatic cities. Accordingly, the first DB branches were established in Bremen (1871) and Hamburg (1872). Both cities had far better and more direct relations with the non-European world, especially with the Americas. However, the first premises of the DB were located in a building on Französische Straße in today's Berlin-Mitte, that is no longer in existence. But as early as 1876 a head office was set up in what was back then Berlin's banking district around Behrensstraße. Today, only one of the two striking arches crossing the streets between the bank's former buildings remains.

One of the first international investments of the fledgling superbank was a stake in a British consortium that bought the Rio Tinto mines in the Spanish province of Huelva in 1873 (see T. Elling, *Andalusia*). The DB, which had quickly developed into the mightiest bank of the newly founded German Empire, soon expanded massively and opened busy branches in Asia and South America. In addition, the company invested heavily in German industry. From 1894 onwards, Frankfurt-born Arthur von Gwinner was a member of DB's Board of Managing Directors, specializing in international connections. He had acquired the necessary know-how during his travels in England and Spain. Under Gwinner, the DB co-financed projects such as the construction of the Baghdad Railway from Turkey to Iraq and grew to become an international player. The Empire generously recognized Gwinner's activities and even granted the man a title. The banker from Frankfurt chose Krumke Castle in Brandenburg's Altmark as his family home. Today, wealthy couples can marry and host parties there.

Germany's history in the first part of the 20th century had little luck in store for the bank, and less for the average German. In 1914 the DB was regarded as one of the most important banks worldwide, but it lost all its international branches in the course of WWI. During the Weimar period the DB was involved in founding and capitalizing new German firms such as the UFA film production company and Lufthansa, but was unable to redevelop its international profile.

In the Third Reich, the DB, along with the entire German economy and industry, was forced (or nudged) into line by the Nazi dictatorship. This led to the dissolving of the DB following Germanys capitulation. Once West Germany had regained some trust and had become a partner of the Western bloc, the bank was re-founded in 1957 as the Deutsche Bank AG, a merger of the West German banks the DB had been split up into after WWII. The new headquarters were set up in Frankfurt. In 1999 the DB officially recognized its historical complicity in the crimes of the Nazis. Today, it is one of the top 20 international banks and the only German bank on the list of systemically important institutions drawn up after the banking crisis of 2007.

> *"Most companies make mistakes when they are doing well, not when they are doing badly."*
>
> *Alfred Herrhausen (1930-1989)*

In West Germany, the re-founded DB successfully transformed itself into a modern company of international standing, notably under the guidance of the influential board member Alfred Herrhausen, who attempted to give the DB an image based on transparency and customer proximity and even went against the general opinion of the financial world by demanding a debt relief for the "Third World" at a World Bank meeting in 1987 (to mind, said concession would have been not all that dramatic for the DB ...).

Considered *"too modern"* by the establishment and international bankers, for German left-wingers Herrhausen was generally *"part of the problem"*, him being the DB's board spokesman and one of its most influential figures. The banker was also regarded as a friend of the then-chancellor Helmut Kohl. This friendship was often quoted as proof of the notion that the German conservative party was basically in cahoots with the rich and mighty of the banking world. A notion that certainly had more than just a ring of truth to it.

In 1989 just after the fall of the Wall, Herrhausen openly spoke out in favor of a rapid reunification. He should not live to see it. Herrhausen became the victim of a bomb attack at the end of November 1989. The German terrorist organization RAF expressed a fairly widespread leftwing view at the time. According to the banker's murderers *"the blood trail of two world wars and the exploitation of millions"* ran through the DB's history. Now, the bank would be *"lurking around, hoping to subject the people (in Eastern Europe) again to the dictates and the logic of capitalist exploitation"*. The "revolutionaries" saw this as sufficient legitimation to kill the banker. But what did they aim to gain? Was it planned and carried out by the "Third Generation" of the RAF alone, which might have hoped to inspire a rebellion of "pan-German anti-fascist forces" or just acted on smug hate, or were further parties involved? The exact identity of perpetrators and organizers was never clarified. But of course, some people quickly suspected that, clearly, the whole thing must have been the handiwork of underground Stasi groups or even the CIA (one can still read relevant theories on websites with *"alternative news"* today: Wall Street, some think, had ordered the CIA to murder Herrhausen because of his proposal to relieve the debts of the Third World countries; the banker was indeed massively criticized for his stance and is even said to have worn a bulletproof vest at a World Bank conference).

In his book *Black Box BRD* author Alexander Veiel quotes former RAF member Birgitt Hogefeld: *"Our willingness*

to escalate this conflict and to embrace military struc-
tures have a much closer connection to the history of
this country than we or at least I have been aware of".
The RAF declared its dissolution in 1998.

In 1992 the DB founded the Alfred Herrhausen Gesellschaft with headquarters in Berlin and premises at *Unter*
den Linden. Its stated aim is to promote a liberal world.
Socialwashing or real concern? After all, the DB is currently regarded as groundbreakingly corrupt by many
Germans, with the growing far-right populists claiming
it was obviously "*bailed out*" by the state using taxpayers' money. But not only the banking crisis damaged
the popular image of the bank. Cases of tax evasion,
climate-negative investments and collusion scandals
have also eaten away at the once "solid" image of the
DB, both at home and abroad.

1871-1918:

Berlin, the imperial city

[Copy of the Flensburger/Idstedter Lion, Heckeshorn, Wannsee island.]

1871 #Schwanenwerder, Colonie Alsen,
Victory Column

Berlin: city of the emperor

Where does one begin to tell the story of the "German
nation" – a wondrous, cruel, twisted tale full of foot-
notes and shame, of ambitions and violent clashes?
One could, with much exaggeration, begin with the
suppression of the Neanderthals at the hand of the
Homo Germanicus, with the mixing with the Celts,
with the protodemocratic assembly (*the Thing*) of the
Germanic tribes with their red hair, already mentioned
by Tacitus; but today, for variety, we start in Spain.
When Queen Isabelle II lost her throne in 1868 in the
course of a revolution little remembered in Germany,
Spain was looking for a new king. Prussia sent a Hohenzollern into the race, the French were opposed, spirits
heated up, and France declared – some believe, at the
instigation of wordsmith Bismarck[20] – war on Prussia,
which dragged the entire North German Confederation
into the conflict. Bismarck had seen an opportunity to
finally create a German nation – not as a consequence
of more or less democratic and revolutionary tendencies in the common people, as had been the danger in
1848, but a nation as the aristocratic powers wanted it

[20] On March 27, 1871 Bismarck received Berlin's honorary citizenship
from a grateful city administration for his services during the founding
of the "Second Reich".

to be born: as a nation given to the German rulers by God and forged in blood.

The southern German states joined the war; the "First Reich", ended by Napoleon, had a successor – the German national empire. During the entire Franco-Prussian War, the diplomats and rulers of the various German states were busy negotiating this entity they already saw wiggling like a sparkling carrot at the end of the bloody tunnel. The German Empire officially came into being before the war was even over, on January 1, 1871. The appointment of the Prussian King Wilhelm I as German Emperor in Versailles' *Hall of Mirrors* a few weeks later had a major propaganda angle. It told everyone who needed to know: the German nation was born in *"Blut und Stahl"* (Blood and Steel), in the enemy's country, in the place so tenderly coveted, envied and imitated by former German royalty. The *Berlin City Palace*, where the Prussian king Friedrich Wilhelm IV had refused to become the emperor of Germany by grace of the "rabble" of the Frankfurt National Assembly in 1849, was now properly made the anchor point of the German Reich. Finally, there was German unity.[21]

[21] One can imagine Prussia before the German Empire a little like a Central European hotchpotch in which various ethnic groups contributed their part to the success of the Prussian enterprise; the most well-known of them being the Polish Prince Radziwill (see *Faust: Almost a preview*); whose relative, Prince Raczinski, saw the foundation of the empire as slightly problematic: *"We could have become Prussians; but we'll never be Germans"*.

The "Great German Empire Show" in Versailles was seen as an affront in France; but this didn't change the outcome of the war. France was defeated, its powers of administration at the mercy of the victors – and very weak. Paris, always good for a revolution, rose up successfully, and the revolutionary *Paris Commune* started to reshape the city along socialist lines. The French central government, horrified by such unbecoming developments, wanted its capital back. So, they swallowed their pride and had a chat with the victorious new German rulers, who released captured French soldiers and generals prematurely so that they could participate in the entailing bloody French civil war. In May 1871, Paris and the *Palais des Tuileries* (once the seat of the French kings, together with what is today the Louvre) were devastated by fire. The ruins of the palace were demolished; items of value were used here and there, and were partly sold.[22] Some parts of the venerable royal home made it to Berlin, to be re-assembled and erected on *Sandtwerder* (Sand Island) in 1884, which was then "developed" and renamed *Schwanenwerder* (Swan Island) – arguably a better name for a higher price tag. *Schwanenwerder* proved to be a magnet for

[22] Recently there have been efforts to rebuild the Palais des Tuileries. The argumentation is very reminiscent of the one made re. the *Berlin City Palace*, i.e. the city would not be the same without it.

[23] After 1945 there was some confusion surrounding the column; it was considered war booty and was to be returned until its legal purchase could be confirmed. The text on the monument reads "*These stones taken from the Seine/planted now in German soil/call warningly to you:/,Fate, how changeable are you.'*"

the rich and powerful. Today, as an inscription on the *Tuileries Column* suggests, it is a good place to reflect on the turmoil of history.[23]

A second monument located not too far away from the *Tuileries Column* fits well into this story: The *Flensburg Lion*. In 1864, the German-Danish War raged, considered the first of the German unification wars. It followed an earlier dispute with the Danish crown during a Silesian uprising, in which Denmark remained victorious. To celebrate Denmark's martial prowess at the Battle of Idstedt[24], a magnificent lion statue was created and then put right in the Old Cemetery in Flensburg. When Flensburg became "German" during the German-Danish War (the population was, as was usual in border areas, very mixed anyway), the German military remembered Napoleon's ill-conceived approach, had the lion dismantled and brought him to Berlin, where he was to inspire young cadets. After the Second World War, the statue was brought to Copenhagen. In 2012, the lion returned to Flensburg – as a symbol of friendship and trust between Germans and Danes and as a reminder of the tragedies caused by nationalist convictions, one would hope.

What does all this have to do with the *Tuileries Column*? Well, there is a morsel of historic parallelism here. In

[24] The lion is named after this victory; when the name *Flensburg Lion* became common is unknown to me.

1863, a villa colony was founded just south of the future Schwanenwerder, and given the name *Alsen* – after the place where the Danish troops surrendered in 1864. A copy of the Flensburg Lion was erected there as some sort of national art in 1874. It is still there, facing the Wannsee.[25]

OK. Berlin's *Siegessäule* (Victory Column) also deserves a mention. It was erected as a monument to the successful military slaughters called *unification wars*. The rings of the column, fashioned from gold-plated cannon barrels, stand for the individual victories.[26] No wonder the CDU politician and ATTAC activist Heiner Geißler described the thing as "*a symbol for nationalism and militarism*" and "*the stupidest monument in Germany*". But still, there are some interesting details; for example, the crowning *Goldelse* (Golden Elsie) was modeled on the daughter of the British Queen Victoria, who, as Victoria Louisa (Else), was the wife of Friedrich III (the 90-day emperor) and thus the German empress. Originally, the *Siegessäule* stood in front of the *Reichstag*, which was built a little later. It was moved to its present location in 1939 as part of some redevelopment work meant

[25] Anyone visiting the Lion should also visit the *House of the Wannsee Conference*, which was where the Nazis first planned in detail the deportation and murder of European Jewry. The bourgeois villa itself, built in 1914, was used by the Nazis as a guest house for the Gestapo.

[26] This is true for the first three rings; the fourth was added by the Nazis when the column was moved from the Reichstag to the centre of the Tiergarten.

to transform Berlin into the world's capital: Germania. Later, the *Siegessäule* gave its name to one of Berlin's leading homosexual magazines (if you need to ask why: don't) and entered the more peaceful side of history as a towering dance pole for numerous Love Parades in the 1990s and as the site of a historic speech by US presidential candidate Barack Obama in 2008. Oh, and the view from under Elsie's skirt is worth the ascent.

1879

[Berlin subway, foto by Anna M. via pexel.com.]

#Main Station, Station Lichterfelde Ost, Subway stations

Siemens and the electro-shy Berliners

Visitors to the 1879 trade exhibition on the premises of the *Lehrter Bahnhof* (today's *Hauptbahnhof* or Main Station) were amazed: Mr. Siemens' new vehicle, presented here for the first time, not only moved without horses, it also did not spout steam! How is that even possible? Simple: The transportation of the future, as Siemens certainly praised his invention, was … electric. Wow! But sadly, the enthusiasm of the Berliners for the electric tram proved to be somewhat ... lukewarm. Siemens, ever the energetic entrepreneur, proposed to build an elevated railway along Friedrichstraße, but the residents were firmly against it, complained, and killed Berlin's chance of having the first electric urban transport system worldwide. Siemens didn't give up, and in 1881 the company was able to set up an electric railway in Lichterfelde: more precisely the world's first publicly used electric tram[27]. The feat is today mentioned by a plaque at the *Bahnhof Lichterfelde-Ost*. In that same year, the Berlin company presented the first electric tram with overhead contact lines in Paris. It was followed in 1883 by *Magnus Volk's Electric Railway* in Brighton, England's first electric tram, which was also powered by a Siemens generator. Volk's Electric Railway still runs along a small stretch of Brighton's beach today; the Lichterfelde tram was mothballed in 1930.

Two Siemens locomotives were also in service on the world's first electrically powered metro line, which began operations in London in 1890. At about the same time, Siemens wanted to set up an electrically powered subway in Berlin. His ambitious plans were thwarted once again, this time due to the city administration's lack of interest. Nevertheless, Siemens built its system in Budapest in 1896, the first continental European electric subway. Berlin's own subway followed in 1902.

[27] Starting in 1874, Fjodor Pirozki had developed a similar project in Russia. Siemens was able to use his results.

It was a high-low railway, still typical of Berlin, connecting the capital with the then independent city of Charlottenburg. The only underground stations were *Potsdamer Platz* (in Berlin), *Wittenbergplatz* and *Zoologischer Garten* (in Charlottenburg).

1880

[Villa Lademann (Neubabelsberg), a Tudor-style building.]

#Lichterfelde

Toy blocks and movie stars

Friedrich Fröbel (the man behind the kindergarten franchise, see above) had the brilliant idea of providing children with geometric wooden blocks to play with – an immediate success in the kindergarten. Gustav Lilienthal (the brother of aviation pioneer Otto Lilienthal) later produced the first blocks mass-made according to measurement standards. The *Anker-Steinbausets*, whose elements could be combined to form e.g. buildings of different architectural styles were produced by the Lilienthals. Due to an unfortunate lack of commercial success, however, Gustav Lilienthal sold the idea in 1880. From 1882 onwards the building blocks were then produced by the Rudolstadt entrepreneur Friedrich Richter, and today they are regarded as the first construction toys; Richter soon issued supplements to the basic Anker set. Between flight tests, the Lilienthals then developed a model construction kit, and received a corresponding patent in 1888. This is considered one of the forerunners of the metal kit. Julius Weiss from Hamburg received the corresponding patent in 1892. The aforementioned Richter company from Rudolstadt again secured the exploitation rights, but this time, success eluded the pioneering toymaker (the *Meccano* set, born in Liverpool in 1908, is considered the world's first successful metal kit).

Two memorial plaques commemorate Gustav Lilienthal in Berlin – one on the *Fliegeberg*, where his work as an aviation pioneer and partner of his brother is honored, and a second on his former residence in Marthastr. 5 in Lichterfelde. More interesting, and more in tune with his architecturally usable building blocks, is the fact that Gustav Lilienthal was also active as an architect. His designs are sometimes called *Lilienthal castles*; with their battlements and oriels they somewhat resemble castles custom-made for well-to-do knights. They boast a "Medieval English" air and can be excellently imitated with the stone building sets Lilienthal fashioned. In 1895, he designed the *Villa Lademann* in Potsdam's Karl-Marx-Str. 66; the house later served as a residence for UFA actors, among them Heinz Rühmann, one of the most popular German film stars of the 1930s. In front of the building, or in front of other similar *Lilienthal castles* in Lichterfelde-West, one might gainfully meditate on the history of building blocks.

#Social Welfare Offices

Bismarck: Stern father of the welfare state?

When Germans discuss the modern welfare state, they usually cite left-wing ideologies, the need for welfare assistance for those less fortunate, and human rights, but they also have a basic conviction in the back of their minds: the whole thing was based on old Bismarck's will to suppress the left wing. It's true: Bismarck's enlightening quote: *"My intention was to win over the working classes, or shall I say, to bribe them, so that they would believe the state to be a social institution working for their benefit and taking care of their well-being"* can be found online as part of the modern emporium of common knowledge, Wikipedia. Things might have changed since then, but the less than perfect pedigree of the social/welfare state proves the suspicions people on the street have concerning the aims of said state to be not entirely unjustified.

However, the Bismarck government invented neither social security nor the welfare state. Still, German social security is the oldest state-regulated system of its kind in the world (health insurance was introduced in 1883, pension schemes in 1889; the unemployment insurance launched in 1927 followed the system introduced in the United Kingdom in 1920). Previously, especially in Prussia, various non-governmental (often with a socialist and therefore, for the ruling powers, dubious background) aid/health insurance funds were already in existence; but we can go even further back. Had Bismarck studied Islam?

The *Rashidun Caliphate*, established in the 7th century shortly after the death of the Prophet Mohamed, used a system reminiscent of the modern welfare state, which financed aid through a kind of tax, the *Zakat* (compulsory alms). What is interesting here is the close connection between power politics/religion and social services. In both cases, the needy were to be strongly bound to a political/ideological power system. By the way, everyone can experience the less attractive sides of the welfare state in Berlin's numerous job centers.

"Germans have a deep need to talk badly about the government while enjoying their beer."

(Otto v. Bismarck)

The electric city

After the American inventor Thomas Alva Edison was awarded his patents on commercially viable light bulbs, the dark side of the world started to develop an electric glow, as everyone wanted to turn night into day. In 1883, entrepreneur Emil Rathenau secured the rights to use Edison's patents in Germany and jump-started the electrical equipment company AEG, which, in addition to illuminating German living rooms in the wake of developments in the US, invented a number of tools that are now indispensable in our lives, including the electric hair dryer (1900) and the magnetic recording tape (1935, Magnetophon K1; OK, this one has since gone the way of the dodo). Following Emil Rathenau's death in 1915, his son Walter took over the management of the company. Walter Rathenau became foreign minister of Germany; due to his assassination organized by an antisemitic/nationalist association in 1922, he is often referred to as the first victim of the Third Reich. Later, the AEG was to come to an arrangement with the Nazis and employed forced laborers. After the Second World War AEG successfully followed up on a patent for the PAL color television system developed by Telefunken (an AEG subsidiary) in Hanover and used in Germany and much of the world. In the mid-1980s, AEG was bought up by Daimler-Benz and finally dissolved in

1996. What remains are memories of various and some-times questionable kinds and the entrance gate to the former *AEG factory* (Brunnenstraße 107).

#Afrikanisches Viertel, Wilhelmstraße, Mohrenstraße

Our place in the sun

When the Hamburg-born minister and later chancellor Bernhardt von Bülow demanded a *"place in the sun"* for the German empire in a speech in 1897, he was not thinking of sun-drenched beaches on which the imperial work force could recover from their toils for the glory of the German industry. Instead, he made it clear that imperial Germany was to end its thus-far restrained foreign policy and would finally get properly into the highly profitable business of colonialism.[28] If the "accepted" European empires could exploit and develop foreign countries, the German "Second Reich", rapping on the gilded doors of the big players and demanding entry like some genius punk who just broke the bank, ought to likewise get a piece of the action. Wilhelm II, who had come to power in 1888, followed von Bülow's demand all too gladly.

---

[28] A short-lived pre-empire colonialism had been in existence from 1683 onwards in Ghana, where the Prussian military had e.g. installed a trade fortress called *Groß Friedrichsburg*. Weapons and other hot products of the time were exchanged for ivory and slaves with the chosen tribe as a trading partner. In 1717, for lack of income, the whole enterprise was sold to the Dutch-West Indian company. The remains of *Groß Friedrichsburg*, together with the trade fortresses of other European powers in West Africa, are today World Cultural Heritage sites.

The Chancellor's statements did not remain without criticism; many members of parliament, especially from the left, were of the opinion that the empire had enough problems at home. But the imperial rulers were hell-bent on the "*adventure*" of colonialism...

It all began a little earlier with the 1884 Congo Conference, organized by Bismarck in an attempt to regulate the "*Scramble for Africa*". On the positive side, the immoral slave trade was then finally defined by treaty as an international criminal offense. At the same time, however, virtually all self-determination options of African political or traditional entities were negated. A plaque in *Wilhelmstraße* commemorates the conference held in the by now long destroyed Reichskanzlerpalais and its dark consequences.

Under Bismarck's leadership, various strategic naval bases had been developed into small settlements. It seems almost anecdotal today that the area around the city of Tsingtao, now Qingdao, was then leased from China in 1897 according to the British model (with gunboat diplomacy) in order to protect German trade interests. Tsingtao grew strongly, since the city offered work and opportunities for advancement. And the brewery *Germania*, founded in Tsingtao in 1903 with British-German capital, ensured liquid bliss. Today, the brewery produces what is likely the most successful internationally marketed Chinese beer under the name *Tsingtao*; it can be found in e.g. almost every Asian supermarket in Berlin and elsewhere. Tsingtao left the area of influence of the German Reich in 1914, when British-Japanese forces took over.

German colonial history quickly mutated into one enormous disaster. Best known is the cruel history of German Southwest Africa; two somewhat dodgy businessmen from Bremen, Adolf Lüderitz and Heinrich Vogelsang, wanted to install a German colony in today's Namibia, which had not yet sparked the imagination of established, professional colonial dreamers, and to make their fortune there. The colony was founded in 1884, when Bismarck imposed a German "protectorate" on the area in reaction to a sudden awakening of an interest in the region in South Africa and Great Britain. A fatal mistake. German Southwest Africa proved to be a powder keg of contradictory aspirations, and the officers and soldiers send to the remote region were either completely overwhelmed by the situation or simply criminals and monsters. The conflict between the German colonial power and the indigenous Herero and Nama in 1904 would become the first genocide of the 20th century, in which General Lothar von Trotha, appointed by the German side, proved himself to be a power seeker and perpetrator of violence of the worst kind – and whose deeds, in retrospect, cast a nasty light on Germany's future. In quotations such as *the use of violence mixed with absolute terrorism and even with cruelty was and is my policy*", the "*great general of the mighty German emperor*" unmistakably expressed his intentions and ambitions. He also introduced "concentration camps" into the German language and military culture: a concept and idea first created a few years earlier by the British in the Boer War as detention centers for members of groups classified as hostile.

"I, the great general of the German soldiers, send this letter to the people of the Herero: The Herero are no longer German subjects ... Within the German borders every Herero ... will be shot ... These are my words to the people of the Herero. Signed: The great general of the mighty emperor."

(Lothar von Trotha, Announcement of the genocide in German Southwest Africa, 1904)

From today's point of view we imagine that the evil imperial German culture simply showed its true face. However, Trotha's actions met with rather vocal criticism in Germany – albeit not immediately, as is customary today. It took official documents and non-wireless communications weeks to get from Namibia to the Reich. The Social Democrats and liberal media criticized the colonial general; even von Bülow, who had demanded Germany's *"place in the sun"*, noted in a message to Emperor Wilhelm II that Trotha's actions violated Christian and human principles, were doomed to failure, and would only damage Germany's reputation. He was right.

"Any butcher's servant can fight a war like Lord von Trotha's."

(August Bebel, Social Democrat, in the Berlin Reichstag, 1904)

The memoirs of the African American civil rights activist W. E. B. Du Bois, who studied in Heidelberg and Berlin from 1892 to 1894, let one hope that at least not all imperial Germans were blindly nationalist and murderously racist individuals. With some surprise, he reported meeting white people in Germany *"who simply shared the present with me. They didn't think of me as an abnormality, or as a subhuman being. I was just a somewhat privileged student they were happy to meet."* Du Bois felt Bismarck had done a great deed in the creation of Germany, as he had formed a nation from different, permanently *"bickering"* groups – the people of the various German states and regions were regarded as very different at the time and likely were so to a degree that we can hardly grasp today – and hoped something similar could happen for African Americans.

The colonial history of Germany ended together with the German Empire. German Southwest Africa became South West Africa and was placed under South African control. The country later changed its name to Namibia after it became independent in 1990. Germany's reputation had been deeply (and rightly so) damaged by the behavior of the imperial military in German Southwest Africa. But in 1919, some political circles in Berlin felt they were treated unfairly; the *Reichskolonialministerium* (Colonial Ministry of the Realm), successor of the *Reichskolonialamt* (Colonial Office of the Realm) created to organize the undoing of colonial ties, even published a comparison between German and British colonial practice, more or less in accordance with the childish

motto: "*They were/are even worse than we ever were!*"
This was preceded by a British publication rightly denouncing the behavior of the imperial German military during the Herero and Nama uprising. Does Germany's contemporary culture of remembrance do better in dealing with this cruel chapter in history? The answer is probably, and as usual, "well – partly". But let's look at a place in Berlin related to this story.

Before WWI, the *Afrikanisches Viertel* (African Quarter) in Wedding was to become a "colonial quarter", to fill Berliners with a certain pride of German "colonial possessions". Zoo director and animal trader Carl Hagenbeck reportedly wanted to set up a large, stationary show of animals and people here (a "human zoo"; a strange institution that enjoyed some popularity in the western world from Berlin to New York). It did not come to that, as German colonialism did not last any real length of time. But the development plan for the area, along with street names, had already been drawn up and prevailed. The "colonial quarter" was built. In addition to the names of the various German colonies, some German colonialists received "streets of honor". In my experience, the history of German colonialism was hardly an issue in West Berlin before 1990. Even today, few Berliners are likely to know that Nachtigalplatz was named not to remind them of Romeo and Juliet, but of Gustav Nachtigal, an Africa researcher and former Reich Commissioner for German West Africa (today Cameroon and Togo).

In 2016 the process of renaming streets honoring people with criminal or questionable colonial connotations began. The new names[29] were finally decided upon at the end of 2018. The Petersallee was to be spilt and called Anna-Mungunda – and Majii-Majii-Allee. The Nachtigalplatz was to become The Manga-Bell-Platz, Lüderitz lost to Cornelius Fredericks. At the behest of interested citizens, the district office wanted to honor "*personalities of the (post-)colonial liberation and emancipation movement from African countries*" (Drucksache 2568/IV). But in spring 2019 it became clear that the project's realization would not be easy. There were historical problems with the Petersallee – it had already been rededicated in 1986, without changing the street name. Following the will of the powers-that-be, the street was to, miraculously, now remind citizens of the politician Hans Peters rather than of the Reichskommissar and colonial criminal Carl Peters, also called *Hänge-Peter* (Hangman Peter). Some believe that this was, well, a tad bogus. Others declare a new, actual renaming to be unnecessary (and cruel to the memory of Hans Peters). Protests were filed. Why? Is it just the cost of new business cards, or do less practical, more sinister convictions lurk in the shadows here? In any case, a typical Berlin trench war seems to be on its way.

Let's consider the Lüderitzstraße; the aforementioned Lüderitz is said to have cheated when buying land from

[29] An article in the Berliner Zeitung reported Queen Nzinga of Ndongo and Matamba as a possible street name. As a powerful woman commanding, as legend has it, a harem full of male sex workers in women's clothes, she seems a cool, independent, even hip. Unfortunately she is also said to have sold slaves from other tribes en masse.

the Nama; his business partners believed they were selling in English miles, but trickster Lüderitz had written the much longer German miles into the contract. This is said to have earned him the nickname *Lügenfritz* (Lying Fritz) in Germany; perhaps a *Lügenfritz-Lüderitz-Straße* would be a suitable, historically relevant new name.

At the corner of Müllerstraße/Otawistraße, an information column has been commemorating this part of history since 2012 – from two perspectives; the more apologetic text on the one side was commissioned by the district parliament, while the other side reflects the view and vocabulary of a citizens' initiative. The difference in tone points to a somewhat very German rift in the interpretation of history, and a visit to the column is worthwhile for this reason alone. It provides a rather simple insight: there is no common German way of viewing German history. The country's colonial history is still a hotly debated topic, even over 100 years later.[30] By the way, modern members of the Trotha family have officially apologized for the deeds of their distant relative and asked for forgiveness. A good, albeit late gesture.

---

[30] In recent years the problematic return of skulls brought to Germany from Africa has been much discussed. During the Herero and Nama uprising, these had been brought to the Charité and other institutions for "*scientific purposes*". Awareness of the problem developed only slowly, and belatedly, despite the occasional eager gesture. When a number of skulls were indeed returned, a representative of the government was booed, and the media reported that Germany had "*embarrassed itself to the bone*". The story continues. In 2016 Berlin officially recognized the actions against the Herero and Nama by colonial Germany as genocide. In 2017 a class action for reparations was filed in New York against the German government by representatives of the Herero and Nama; the lawsuit was dismissed in 2019.

And at this point a brief foray: in 1908, Chancellor von Bülow advocated a memorial to be erected in Berlin for the Germans who died in the colonies, including those who fought (and killed) during the conflict with the Herero and Nama. Never implemented in Berlin, the design served as a model for a colonial monument erected in Bremen not far from the main train station in 1932. It is a strangely charming, large African brick elephant in the middle of a green northern German lawn. Bremen, which had profited massively from the colonial adventure, looked back at the colonial times with a tear in its eye. The city fondly remembered its son Lüderitz, and duly commemorated the German victims ... But times changed. In 1989, the elephant was re-dedicated as an anti-colonial monument, as part of a European campaign against apartheid. Today, it commemorates the victims of German colonial policy. In 2009, a monument to the victims of Trotha's war against the Nama and Ovaherero was installed right next to the anti-colonial monument; and in 2014 the park in which both monuments are located was named after the then recently deceased Nelson Mandela. It seems the city found a way to clearly point at the elephant in the room (without destroying it).

Breaking Bad

When the chemist Lazar Edeleanu[31], who came to Berlin from his native Romania, successfully completed the first synthesis of amphetamine (in addition to its real name, the substance, which is used for various medicinal purposes including the treatment of hyperactivity disorders, is also known as the illegal stimulant *speed*) at the University of Berlin, hardly anyone had any idea what uses his innocation would come to have. Especially the related methamphetamine, synthesized shortly afterwards in Japan by Nagayoshi Nagai and Akira Ogata, for which Berlin pharmaceuticals company Temmler secured a manufacturing patent in 1934, was to gain, well, historic significance. Introduced to the market for uppers as *Pervitin*, it was used to improve mental and physical performance and combat symptoms of fatigue, i.e. just what the Wehrmacht needed. The compound, soon popularly known under various names including *Panzerschokolade* (tank chocolate), was purchased by the million by the army administration. Nazi Germany's soldiers duly showed "high" performance levels during

[31] Today Edeleanu is mainly known as the developer of the first modern process for refining crude oil (1908, Edeleanu process for sulphur dioxide extraction, developed in Romania). Edelenau, who had Jewish ancestors, founded the *Allgemeine Gesellschaft für Chemische Industrie* in Germany in 1910, which he later had to sell to an "Aryan" company. He escaped the Nazis and died during WWII in Bucharest.

the Blitzkrieg. In high doses, the addictive drug is said to lead to disinhibition.

Pervitin was produced in West Germany until 1988 – and the armies of both German countries always held a certain supply ready. I guess you just never know. But it was not only the German army who was interested in the combat-enhancing drug; US soldiers are also said to have used the drug as a miracle weapon. From zero to super soldier in no time flat (anyone thinking of Captain America here?).

> *"Could you could get me some more Pervitin for my provisions?"*
>
> *(Heinrich Böll in his field post, 1940)*

The question is, of course, whether the industrially produced Pervitin could compete with the cultural legacy of the famous chemistry teacher in the mainstream US series *Breaking Bad*. After all, methamphetamine is nothing short of controlled crystal meth.[32]

---

[32] The drug found its way into US TV by way of the chemist Steve Preisler, also known as Uncle Fester (named after a character from the TV series *The Addams Family* who likes to blow things up). Preisler published his successful book *Secrets of Methampethamine Manufacture* in the 1980s; the title says it all. Preisler also wrote books on nerve gas, LSD and weapons.

The Banker, the Heavens and Berlin

The Nasrid rulers, who created the Alhambra in the early 14th century in what was then Moorish Granada, could hardly have dreamed that one day a piece of their palace would find its way into the veritable hamlet that Berlin was in around 1300. In fact, hardly anyone in Granada believes this possible even today; and when one reveals to the inhabitants of that beautiful and proud city that a ceiling taken from the Alhambra is exhibited in a Berlin museum, the legitimacy of the acquisition is immediately questioned. After all, Ferdinand & Isabella aka the Catholic Monarchs had conquered the Alhambra fair and square, ceiling and all. How did those Berliners scam Granada out of its possession? No Berliner did. It was a banker from Frankfurt.

This story somehow begins with the American writer Washington Irving, who enjoyed the status of a best-selling author in the early 19th century. He wanted to top his hugely successful heroic biography of the discoverer Christopher Columbus with a work detailing the reconquest of Granada. After all, Columbus was given the task, if you like, of discovering the New World near or in Granada following said reconquest. Irving travelled to Granada on research, where he was given rooms in the famous Moorish fortress. In 1829, he wrote his Tales of the *Alhambra* there. The popular book led to a kind of *Alhambramania* in the finer circles of the industrialized world. In 1851, a replica of the Lion Court of the Alhambra was installed in London for the first world exhibition at the Crystal Palace (and then until 1936 in the permanent and enlarged Crystal Palace, an amusement park in Sydenham). This exhibit might well have been seen by Frankfurt banker Arthur von Gwinner (whom we have already met in the chapter on the *Deutsche Bank*) during his time in London.

In 1880, Gwinner was working for a French bank in Madrid and as an Honorary Consul of the German Reich in Spain. In 1882 he visited Granada, which, due to its Moorish heritage and Irving's book along with other works and exhibitions on the subject, had by then earned the reputation of a lost paradise. The Alhambra itself was not in the best condition. Some fortifications had been blown up by the departing Napoleonic army in 1812. Furthermore there was damage from an earthquake, and the Spanish crown was chronically short of cash, so repairs had to wait. Irving described the place, with all its magic, as clearly *"gnawed at by the ravages of time"* and reported numerous collapsed towers. Habitable parts of the Alhambra were leased or sold to private individuals, who then oversaw the preservation of the premises. At the time of Gwinner's visit, the opera singer Modesto Lluch lived in the Torre de las Damas, an important part of the Partal, the northernmost part of the Nasrid Palace. Gwinner, who immediately succumbed to the magic of the Alhambra, acquired Lluch's lease and even bought the building and the surrounding gardens in 1886. It should not be overlooked that, even in those distant days, some attentive citizens of Granada complained about the sale.

The busy and comparatively loaded banker didn't spend much time in his Andalusian property. He got married in the same year and then spent his honeymoon, appropriately, in Granada, making plans to restore the original structure of the Partal – which had likely been adapted to the purposes of its various inhabitants – and even considered moving the whole thing to Berlin, where he was to work next. Around 1888, he had the ceiling of the Torre de las Damas transplanted to his house in Berlin. In 1891, he donated the Torre de las Damas to the Spanish State – albeit without the original ceiling – and had a plaque affixed to the structure, to draw attention to his generous donation. If you dig a little deeper, however, it seems more complicated. The Torre de las Damas was likely sold or leased for the first time in 1828. In 1879, even before the purchase by Gwinner, a law was passed to expropriate owners of properties deemed of national interest. The Alhambra itself had been declared a national monument in 1870. As a businessman with a clear sense for his options, Gwinner wouldn't have hoped to keep the Torre de las Damas as his property, or even move it to Germany. The removal of the ceiling could have been a clever compromise with the responsible authorities. In his Berlin apartment, the ceiling was supposed to remind him of his, in all reality, short stint in Granada for the rest of his life; at the same time, he followed the trend of the rich and fashionable Europe of his day and showed his abundant wealth by flashing the "oriental" style.

After WWII, Gwinner's descendants brought the ceiling to West Germany and offered it to the *Patronato de la Alhambra* in 1978 – but the Spanish government refused the requested funds for repurchase, probably for lack of money. After all, in 1964, a good and far from cheap replica of the ceiling had been installed in the Torre de las Damas, and was considered original by all those inexperienced first-time visitors and most other passers-by. The genuine ceiling was subsequently sold to the *Islamic Art Museum* in Berlin-Dahlem; it then became a part of the collection of the *Pergamon Museum* in 2000, where it bears witness to Europe's fascination for the East and occupies a place of honor among other masterpieces of Islamic art. Incidentally, the stalactite dome ceilings of the Alhambra are supposed to represent the sky according to the Quran. Personally, I find it reassuring to know that God's heaven, with all its implications and demands, is now a museum exhibit (although, side note: the ceiling in question is a wood carving and might have some other meaning).

The influence of the Alhambra, or of the orientalism of the late 19th century, can also be felt, at least possibly, in the New Synagogue on Oranienburger Straße. It is often said that Eduard Knoblauch, a celebrated Berlin architect with Hungarian roots, used the Alhambra as a model for the religious structure, which, as we have seen earlier, was by no means unusual at the time. The book *Plans, Elevations, Sections and Details of the Alhambra* by the English architect Owen Jones was widely known, the Moorish style popular and almost ubiquitous. There seems to be no evidence that Knoblauch ever visited the Alhambra. In addition, there is another possible source of inspiration – the interests of Knoblauch's mentor, Friedrich Schinkel, in Indian architecture. Either way: the New Synagogue was extremely popular with con-temporary Berliners. There were reports of a *"magical transfiguration"*; some people raved about the *"fairy-tale effect"*. The self-confident depiction of the impor-tance of Judaism, however, also aroused anti-Semitic voices demanding that all buildings in Germany should be erected *"in the German architectural style"*; these upstanding citizens would surely have left the disputed ceiling (see above) in the Torre de las Damas.

[Lilienthal monument, Fliegeberg, Lichterfelde.]

#Fliegeberg, Gollenberg

What a strange bird man is ...

The world, they say, has become smaller. And yes, the time distances between the waiting room and the exit hall of two airports in different countries or even on distant continents are actually relatively short. All this is made possible by the principles of movement in and through the air via the application of force (in contrast to slower forms of air travel such as e.g. floating around in balloons). Otto Lilienthal from Anklam is regarded as one of the pioneers of this technique, which has had a decisive impact on our modern world (just think of the increasing number of almost identical photographs of the Brandenburg Gate, scattered around Europe, aye, around the globe thanks to low-cost airlines, and, yes, of the climate crisis).

Lilienthal, who hailed from a rather poor background, almost became an American – but alas, his father died shortly before he could lead his family to the USA, where he had hoped to find a better life for himself, his wife and his two sons. Whether Otto and his brother Gustav would have become interested in flight in, say, New York remains unknown – but in Brandenburg, they were fascinated by the many avian species swishing through the Prussian airspace. Later on, Otto was able to secure an internship with the Berliner machine factory Schwartzkopff in the *Feuerland* (burning country) and received a scholarship to study at the Gewerbeakademie Berlin. From 1874 at the latest, he explored the advantage of curved wings over flat ones, and in 1889 published his classic book *Der Vogelflug als Basis der Fliegekunst* (Birdflight as the Basis for Aviation). A milestone? Today, it is certainly considered as such. But at the time of publication, his book enjoyed little coverage – and was in any case not groundbreakingly new. Frenchman Louis Mouillard, who had worked in Egypt, had already written a book with similar ideas a few years earlier.

But Otto Lilienthal didn't stop there, and he set about things systematically. He behaved like an orphaned young bird, testing his abilities by jumping and gliding off platforms and hills with various self-constructed apparatuses. From 1893 onwards he undertook flight tests on the Gollenberg in Havelland and on an artificial mound in today's Lichterfelde Süd (then outside Berlin), the *Fliegeberg* (Aviators Mountain). He undertook countless test flights, gliding up to 80 meters through the air after jumping off the *Fliegeberg*; in 1932, a monument was inaugurated here in his honor. Being an entrepreneur, Lilienthal offered the standard glider he developed and used for test purposes for sale from 1894 onwards – *"for the practice of aerobatics"*, according to the original advertising. The production site of this first aircraft for the general market was located at 113 Köpenicker Straße (see the memorial pillar outside the building). The production volume was minimal, but Berlin may, with some right, proudly call itself *"Home of commercially produced solo aircraft"*. Talking of entrepreneurs: Lilienthal had another good idea back in 1890. To encourage the employees of his factory to improve their output and show more interest in their work, he introduced a profit-sharing scheme – a great incentive today mainly offered to executives.

In the meantime, the world had become aware of the aviator; pictures of the gravity-defying Berliner were published around the globe, while his numerous essays were translated into various languages. The skies were wide open ... But on August 9th, 1896, Otto Lilienthal crashed during a test flight at Gollenberg in the Havelland; it is assumed unfortunate air currents were responsible. A day later he succumbed to his wounds.

"The flight of men ... will give us eternal peace ..."

(Otto Lilienthal)

Today, a large sculpture on the Gollenberg, the Wind-harfe (Wind Harp), reminds visitors of these early human flights. In addition, there is an area close by dubbed the "world's oldest airfield" in memory of Lilienthal. Regular take-offs and landings, albeit with leg propulsion, were carried out here early on. There is an active runway operated by an aviation club and the Lilienthal Center (its attraction is a long-haul aircraft of the state airline of the GDR named after Lilienthal's wife Agnes, which had landed here in 1989 and now serves as a museum and as a registry office for romantically inclined aviators).

Lilienthal's influence was enormous and also clearly recognized by the pioneers who followed him. The American aviation pioneer Wilbur Wright, who, together with his brother, advanced Lilienthal's work decisively, wrote: "*(Lilienthal) set forth the advantages of arched wings in such convincing manner as to make him the real originator of this feature.*" But despite his powers of observation and his sharp mind, Otto Lilienthal was thoroughly mistaken regarding the importance of the "art of flying" for the 20th century. He wrote: "*The borders between countries would lose their significance ... National defense, because it has become*

---

[33] Berlin-Tempelhof is often called the „mother of all airports", but it was certainly not the first one. The College Park Airport in Maryland, USA is most often considered the oldest airport; it was opened by Wilbur Wright in 1909. While flight demonstrations took place on the Tempelhofer Feld that same year, the airport there was not officially established until 1923.

impossible, would stop devouring the best resources of the state, and there will be a compelling need to resolve nations' disputes in some other way ... the art of flying will give us eternal peace." It's nice to think that such a clever mind simply couldn't imagine the then not-so-distant world of Göring and Arthur "Bomber" Harris.

A quantum of knowledge ...

In the late 19th century the electrical industry was one of the most important technology sectors in the world – and Werner Siemens, a native of Lower Saxony, was one of its pioneers. Electrical engineering requires precise measurements in well-defined systems. Siemens, together with physicist Hermann von Helmholtz, called for the establishment of an institute for developing measurement methods, in other words, of a metrology institute. After lengthy hesitation, the German Reichstag decided to establish the *Physikalisch-Technische Reichsanstalt* in 1887, with Helmholtz as its first president; Siemens supplied premises in Berlin-Charlottenburg. One of the first tasks of the new institute was to answer a practical question: would it be more economical to light the booming city of Berlin with electric or gas-powered lamps? In order provide a well-founded answer, a suitable light intensity standard had to be defined; and the *Physikalisch-Technische Reichsanstalt* was more than up to the task. Its efforts from 1895 onwards led to the development of the world's first cavity radiator and to measurements with unprecedented accuracy, which contradicted previous attempts to explain thermal radiation. For scientists, little is more stimulating than results that do not correspond with predictions ...

Immediately, many clever minds heated up as they stared into nearby light sources. It was Max Planck who suggested that, on the basis of the measurements, it should be assumed that electromagnetic energy is only emitted in discrete quanta. Planck's perhaps somewhat grudging bow to the mensurations related to the cost-effectiveness of Berlin's street lighting then started the avalanche of quantum physics.[34] Werner Heisenberg described Planck as *"a conservative spirit"* who told his son during walks in the Grunewald about his dubitations on what he believed to be necessary conclusions. At the end of 1900, however, he finally published his findings. Albert Einstein, a rather non-conservative spirit, then continued on Planck's path, but would, in a twist of fate, later often doubt the predictions of quantum mechanics.

To recall the birth of quantum physics, I propose one of the most enchanted and underrated places in Berlin: the open-air gas lantern museum in the Tiergarten, near the S-Bahn station Tiergarten. At night it is a magical place (at least if a good number of the lamps work – there seems to be much vandalism going on in Berlin), boasting different models of lamps from various German and European cities. Among them is one from Copenhagen; the Danish capital was to become an important transit point in the history of the natural sciences through the "Copenhagen interpretation" of quantum mechanics in 1927.

[34] A slightly related story: In 1889 Berlin's *Verein für Eisenbahnkunde* (Railroad Association) demanded the introduction of a standard time for railway services in Germany, hinting at the sound experiences other countries had already made with this practice. Britain, the first country to do so, had introduced Railway Time in 1840. In Germany cities still used local railway times. In 1893 a universal time was introduced for the entire German Empire (the northern German railways had been using a unified time zone since 1874) based on the 15th meridian running through the city of Görlitz. Perhaps a moment a young Einstein noted with interest at the time.

Before I forget: despite constant efforts to harmonize street lighting to electric light, Berlin is still the city with most gas lanterns internationally (Frohnau has the world's largest continuous area illuminated by gas lanterns). The decision on the cost-effectiveness of lighting methods is likely to have been made accordingly. Currently (2019) about 30,000 of Berlin's 224,000 street lamps are gas lamps. However, to help save the planet and the environment, these are slowly being retrofitted. Nevertheless, around 3,000 gas lamps are to be preserved as an area monument.

And the Physikalisch-Technische Reichsanstalt? It quickly gained a superb reputation; James Chadwick (who proved the existence of the neutron in England in 1932) and Hans Geiger[35], for example, conducted research in the field of radioactivity at the Reichsanstalt in around 1914.

[35] Hans Geiger did not stay in Berlin forever. In 1925 he went to the University of Kiel as professor, where he developed the Geiger counter (Geiger-Müller counter, after Geiger and his colleague Walther Müller). He later returned to Berlin, where he played a role in nuclear energy research during the Weimar period and the Nazi dictatorship. He died in Berlin in 1945 and was buried in Potsdam. The Wikipedia entry (2018) on Geiger claims the existence of a second grave with his name in the Grunewald cemetery on a *Gleisinsel* (railroad island) near the Halensee train station (some Berliners call the place *Toteninsel*, the island of the Dead; a fitting name). The given reason is that his family moved to the West after the division of Germany and had another gravestone erected, for proximity. Nice story, but ... I couldn't find the stone, and not even the helpful cemetery workers could locate it. But the story is too fantastic and apt not to be mentioned. The small cemetery is therefore well suited to reflect on the riddles of quantum mechanics, on catty Schrödinger's graves and the truth of what one reads.

#Bahnhof Friedrichstraße

Kangaroos in winter's garden

The path to what we call cinema, and to our uncanny ability to exchange reality for its mostly none-too-accurate representation in the dark, was full of bends and loops, fragmented and marked by parallel developments. While the first film camera in history was constructed around 1888 by the Frenchman Louis Le Prince in Leeds, England, the brothers Max and Emil Skladanowsky from Pankow followed in 1894 with their *Kurbelkiste I* (crank case I).

In 1887, a cutting-edge vaudeville stage opened in Berlin-Mitte with the aim of rivaling the best (Viennese) venues of its kind and a burning ambition to go even further: the *Wintergarten* (winter garden), part of the fashionable Central-Hotel, located directly next to the Bahnhof Friedrichstraße. Here, the rich and famous of Berlin mingled and demanded to be tuned into the mad, raving pulse of time. Along came the Skladanowskys

[36] The first film projector was developed by the Briton Eadweard Muybridge back in 1879, followed by a corresponding apparatus by the aforementioned Louis Le Prince.

with their films. As a natural complement to the *Kurbelkiste*, they had created another cinematic apparatus: the *Bioskop* projector.[36]

Starting on November 1, 1895 this ingenious contraption projected films onto a canvas after real dancers (and other artists) had performed their show. The Skladanowskys showed the amazed audience brief footage from real life, including scenes such as *The Boxing Kangaroo* and *Acrobatic Potpourri* (recorded live in Moabit; the audience could have seen it there, but seeing a second-hand representation on a flat screen was considered more hip, in time, rad or "way to go"). Thanks to the boxing kangaroo, the Wintergarten[37] had become the world's first regular cinema – even if only for a few minutes and at the end of a variety show.

Max Skladanowsky then travelled across Europe with his *Bioscope* and enjoyed great success – but the projector that ultimately proved to be more important for the evolution of cinema was the technically superior apparatus of the Lumière brothers. Its first public use likewise fell in 1895. In December of that great first

[37] The Central-Hotel was destroyed in a bombing raid during WWII; taking its place, a rather faceless building is currently taking up the space next to the Friedrichstraße station. As a Berlin celebrity, the Varieté Wintergarten was nevertheless to be reborn; in 1992 it was revived in the rooms of the former Quartier Latin, known for pop and rock concerts during the 1980s, and now a place for those willing to spend a few more bucks for a night out.

cinematic year, interested Parisians saw short films of the Lumières in the Grand Café on the Boulevard des Capucines – as rumor has it, in the presence of the Skladanowsky brothers. In 1897, after a final performance in Stettin/Szczecin[38], the Skladanovskys gave up touring with the *Bioscope*, which can now be marveled at in the Potsdam Film Museum.

---

[38] In Szczecin, at the time considered "Berlin's port", a small building is billed as the world's oldest cinema. Founded in 1907 as the *Helios-Welt-Kino-Theater*, it survived WWII and then entertained the new Polish population under the name *Kino Odra*. It is now called *Kino Pionier*. But is this really the oldest cinema still active? The Berlin cinema *Moviemento* (Zickenplatz) likewise opened its doors in 1907 (originally named *Kino Topp* after the operator, a certain Mr. Topp – hence the German term *Kintopp* for movies). But we may have to further our search. In 1897 the *Roxburgh Cinema* is said to have opened in Roxburgh, New Zealand (there are rumors that it was discontinued and reopened in 1930; whoever passes by there: please have a look). And of course there is the *Eden* in the small French town of La Ciotat; the Lumières held an event there in 1899, often regarded as the first real cinema show; it closed its gates in 1982, but was reopened in 2013.

1897

The stony road to sexual freedom

In Charlottenburg, in 1897 not yet part of Berlin, the friends Magnus Hirschfeld, Max Spohr, Eduard Oberg and Franz Joseph von Bülow founded the *Wissenschaftlich-Humanitäres Komitee* (Scientific-Humanitarian Committee) with the aim of decriminalizing sexual acts between men. In 1872, Section 175 of the German Penal Code had come into force, stating that *"the unnatural fornication committed between persons of the male sex or by persons with animals is to be punished with prison, and/ or by withdrawal of civil rights"*. Signatures were collected and, after mediation by the Social Democrats, a petition was submitted to the Reichstag – albeit in vain. The *Komitee* was, however, likely the first association to campaign for the equality of homosexuals in society.

Magnus Hirschfeld, who introduced the term *transvestite* in 1910, founded the world's first institution for sexual research in 1919. The research stock of the institute was mainly a library, which was destroyed by the Nazis during their burning of books. Also in 1919, Hirschfeld appeared alongside actor Conrad Veidt in the feature film *Anders als die Anderen* (Unlike the Others). The film, the first to address homosexuality directly, could be screened at the time since no censorship was exercised in the Weimar Republic from 1918-1920; immediately after the introduction of film censorship in 1920, *Anders als die Anderen* was banned. Hirschfeld, a Jewish German, left Germany in the early 1930s; he died in French exile in 1935.

Today, a section of the riverbank in Moabit near his former place of residence bears his name, and a memorial stone commemorates his work. In 2011, the German government set up the *Magnus Hirschfeld Federal Foundation*, which has the aim of combatting the discrimination of homosexuals.

Incidentally, Section 175 continued to apply for a long time in West and East Germany, even if in a diluted form – until 1988 in the GDR, in the FRG and the newly united Germany until 1994.

"Humans are, if anything, born unequal."

(Magnus Hirschfeld)

/_ _ _/

1904

American Samuel Morse and his collaborator Alfred Vail laid the foundations for morse telegraphy in the 1830s by inventing an electromagnetic device for transmitting impulses and a corresponding code; it is not known if they immediately thought their code would be used for naval distress signals (or for clandestine communications among earthlings jailed by extraterrestrials, a concept particularly popular in sci-fi movies – it seems the morse code, albeit almost forgotten by everybody else, is well present in the brains of almost all interstellar heroes; the code used by these interstellar morse buffs is likely the variant adapted by the Friedrich Gerke, which was declared the international morse code in Paris in 1865). For a long time there was indeed no uniform emergency call signal among morse users. The companies that dominated the telegraph business – Marconi in London and Telefunken in Berlin – used their own emergency signals and are said to have even prohibited their radio operators from listening to the traffic of the "other side", i.e. from adjusting their receivers to those bad, bad frequencies used by the competition.

In 1904, the German navy came up with the idea of using a uniform, concise tone sequence as an emergency call signal: a tone sequence so striking that it would easily be noticed in the cacophony of radio signals. So catchy, in fact, that even heroes near distant stars in the cubicles of mean green aggressors would still know them (OK, the imperial admiralty might not have thought all that far – but still).

They agreed on the sound sequence Short Short Short – Long Long Long – Short Short Short, which, translated from morse code, means "SOS". This was, by the way, no abbreviation (such as the often claimed Save Our Souls), but simply a concise, poignant and otherwise hardly ever occurring code sequence. The decision was made by the imperial navy (where and when exactly the relevant meeting took place is unknown, but its headquarters were in Berlin), but caught on only slowly. The radio operator of the ill-fated Titanic is said to have been one of the first to use it, alerted by an informed colleague, but we all know how that story ended.

Oh, and German pop heroes also used the morse code. Among many other musicians, the band *Kraftwerk* found it interesting to actually express meaning with simple tones, or even translate lyrics into such tones, as they did for their song *Radioaktivität* from 1975; in a remix from 1991, the "SOS" is used extensively. Hm. Should it be that simple? Could it be that the futuristic heroes in distress mentioned earlier are, were or will be enthusiastic nerd fans of the historic band *Kraftwerk* (and therefore fondly remember the tonal works of the German navy)?

Flash! Aaaahaaa ...

The battery is another thing without which our world would be a completely different one, supplying portable electronics with electricity and therefore us with music or light, as in the case of the flashlight. Georges Leclanché can justifiably be called the grandfather of the battery. His Leclanché element worked with liquid electrolyte (it was a so-called "wet battery"). Although it was somewhat mobile, however, one would have needed a push cart to use it as a walkman – the thing was rather heavy. In 1886, Carl Gassner in Mainz received a patent for an improved dry cell battery. This may have inspired the British inventor David Misell. In 1899, he was awarded the first patent for a battery-powered torch, in which three batteries were inserted one after the other, and then signed it over to the predecessor of the American company Everready. What does all this have to do with Berlin? Paul Schmidt, born in Köthen, Germany, was one of the many inventors working on moving the dry cell battery along towards mass production – and received a patent for his improvements in 1896. In 1901, Schmidt developed the flat battery (not quite quantum mechanics, it's simply three 1.5 V batteries connected to form a 4.5 V battery in a common casing). Under the brand name DAIMON Schmidt's battery trio would become known in Germany as well as worldwide. In 1906, Schmidt registered a patent for an improved electric torch. Since 2016, he and his batteries have been commemorated in a small museum in Hohenschönhausen, in a house Paul Schmidt and his family inhabited for many years. Visitors can admire numerous historical batteries, as well as a particularly portable torch model introduced in 1937 under the name "handy" (German for mobile phone). Needless to say, he is locally considered the flat-out inventor of the flashlight.

The modern condom

The history of the condom is long; even back in the 18th century, condoms from animal intestines protected consenting adults from dangerous venereal diseases such as syphilis, and from unwanted pregnancies. The 19th century saw Charles Goodyear, the great pioneer of the rubber industry, produce the first rubber condoms, but they still had a not-so-pleasant seam. The modern, seamless condom was then developed by Julius Fromm in Berlin in 1912. Perhaps just a detail, but who would consider using a sewn condom today?

Fromm was not born in Berlin. He hailed from Konin (then part of the Russian Empire, now Poland), from where his family moved to Berlin's Scheunenviertel in search of a better future. For years, Fromm made a living by rolling and selling cigarettes at home while at the same time studying chemistry in evening classes. During his experiments with rubber, Fromm came up with the ingeniously simple idea of dipping a glass bulb in a raw rubber solution, before removing it and allowing it to cool. Tataa, a new condom was born. At first, he produced and peddled his product as a one-man-factory, but the high demand (*"Hand me a seamless Fromm special and I'll show you a good time"*, said the spider to the sexy flies) made bigger things possible. In 1916, Fromm, now an entrepreneur, introduced *Fromms Act* as a brand into Berlin's condom market; "Fromms" became a common term for condoms in Germany for decades to come – which some found funny, as his name means "pious" in German.

The world's first purpose-built condom factory went into operation in Berlin-Friedrichshagen in 1922. By 1929, production capacity had reached its limits and had to be expanded – which led to the construction of one of the first-ever factory buildings in the style of the *Neue Sachlichkeit* ("New Objectivity"; the architect was Arthur Korn from Breslau/Wroclaw) on Friedrichshagener Straße in Köpenick. It was made entirely of steel, concrete and glass. The last remnants of Fromm's factory were demolished in 2007, and the site is now occupied by a standard DIY superstore. But back to our story …

Fromm became rich, bought a villa and founded companies abroad. But then, the Nazis came to power. Fromm, of Jewish descent, initially tried to resist the subsequent pressure and harassment, but soon realized he had no chance in the "new" Germany. He was forced to sell his company to a relative of Hermann Göring at a price far below its value. Fromm went to London, where he died shortly after the war ended. In the soon-founded GDR, an attempt by one of his relatives to reclaim the factory for his family was stopped; the GDR authorities regarded

Fromm as a "capitalist exploiter" who had made lucrative deals with the Nazi government. Fromm's factory was converted into public property under the War Crimes Assets Confiscation Act. In October 2014, a *Stolperstein* (memorial stone set into the sidewalk) was installed at the site of Fromm's factory; the costs were covered by the local DIY superstore.

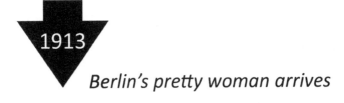

1913

Berlin's pretty woman arrives

There are many stories and many contradictory, often politically charged opinions about how the bust of Nefertiti made its way into a Berlin museum and into the hearts of (most) Berliners. All these stories have a common starting point: Achetaton, on the banks of the Nile, where the couple Akhenaton and Nefertiti ruled as happy demigods – even if only briefly. Their empire, a controversial interlude in Egyptian history, fell into pretty absolute oblivion until Napoleon wanted to free the French Republic of Cairo from the British yoke and, since he was at it, gave birth to the modern excavation craze in Egypt. The area of lost Achetaton was some time later mapped by the founder of British Egyptology, John Gardner Wilkinson. Under the name Tell el-Amara it became a popular playground for international excavation efforts, which soon were en vogue among the upper classes – it was something one simply had to support to have any leeway at dinner parties.

Financially helped along by Berlin cotton merchant James Simon and on behalf of the *German Oriental Society* (DOG), Ludwig Borchardt searched for hidden treasures at Tell el-Amara in the early 20th century. The DOG was founded in Berlin in 1898 and, following British and French efforts, wanted to contribute to the discovery and preservation of finds from the distant past.

During his excavations, Borchardt came across the studio of one Thutmosis – and the bust of Nefertiti. He also found other treasures, of course, but Nefertiti was ... different. Today, many people wonder, especially in the upper office floors of the Egyptian Museum in Cairo, why this special treasure did not stay in its home country. In 2011 the head of the Egyptian Antiquities Administration asked for the bust to be returned (this was not the first such demand). Borchardt, and thus Berlin, had scammed the masterpiece, they argued. But let's take this step by step.

At the start of the 20th century, such excavations were usually divided by way of a system called *partage*. The find in question comprised about 400 items and was accordingly divided into two lots of 200 pieces each – one of which would go to the land of the excavation, the other to the financier. So far, so fair. Funky detail: at that time Egypt was occupied by the British, and the country's antiquities service was – traditionally, see Napoleon – under French leadership. Meaning: a Frenchman had the choice between the two batches – one with, and one without the Nefertiti.[39]

[39] As early as 1914 the regulation in force was changed; from that year onwards all unique pieces had to remain in Egypt (as the Nefertiti was not a star yet then, her case is likely unconnected). Until then, as trickster Borchardt likely did, one could secure a valuable specimen by skillfully dividing the lots, which was a right reserved for the excavating party.

Borchardt is said to have regarded the bust of Nefertiti as something very unique, and to have made special efforts to secure the bust for his financier, James Simon. Some say he secretly smeared it with clay or intentionally dimmed the light in its exhibition space so as to obscure the unusual colors; others think he gave unacceptable quantities of wine to the French decision-maker to cloud his mind. The most likely version is that he cunningly added a treasure even more desirable for the Egyptian side to the other lot: a folding altar with a depiction of Nefertiti, Akhenaton and three of their children. Borchardt described this altar in a 1913 DOG newsletter as follows: *"Outside the building a very important find was made: a completely painted limestone stela ... a charming genre work of the royal family ... I think it's fair to say there's no other depiction of the royal family of higher quality from that time"*. Today, the stela is exhibited in the Egyptian Museum in Cairo. The bust of Nefertiti found in the same excavation is discussed in Borchards official missives, but described somewhat less enthusiastically. Borchardt reports that he also found a preliminary version of the portrait bust in which the face is too full, too *"healthy"*. He remarks on some *"sickly"* traits around the eye: *"Thutmes then highlighted the necessary corrections with a firm black brush stroke and restarted the portrait model, this time with complete success."* Borchardt also expressed his satisfaction that, in the sharing of the finds, it had been possible to achieve an allocation of *"scientifically valuable"* subsets thanks to the sound work done by the selecting officials. Yet, some claim that Borchardt himself forged the folding altar at home in order to offer the other side something even more desirable than the royal bust.

In any case, Nefertiti, who was granted an official exit permit in 1913, came to Berlin and jumped right onto James Simon's desk, where the handsome woman delighted visitors such as Kaiser Wilhelm. Borchardt immediately spoke out against presenting the bust to the public – was he afraid his charade would be noticed? Anyway, Simon, every inch a patron of the arts, gave the bust to the Free State of Prussia, after having kept her on his desk for a good ten years. It became state property and was presented to the public for the first time on the Museum Island in 1924. The Nefertiti quickly achieved fame as Berlin's most beautiful woman. And somehow, the bust looks not unlike the ideal image of a Berlin woman of the 1920s: bold features, cool, self-confident. Some even claim that she looks amazingly similar to Borchardt's wife in her salad days. Wait a minute. Is Nefertiti a fake? Had prankster Borchardt forged not the altar the Egyptians kept, but Nefertiti?

The real question is: Does it matter? No – because she's a star. A solitaire, something special. The Nefertiti hype that began in 1924 soon led to claims for restitution by Pierre Lacau, head of the Egyptian antiques service since 1914. The Frenchman was hardly fond of the Germans, whom he liked to call "*les boches*", and cited a moral dimension; he likely made the first accusations that the "*boches*" had fraudulently appropriated the Nefertiti. Berlin museum officials didn't want to leave the elephant in the room.

In 1929, Lacau was able to arrange a barter with the then director of the Egyptian Museum in Berlin; he would be allowed to bring Nefertiti back to Egypt, for which the Berlin museum would receive two valuable statues. James Simon nodded his approval. Berliners back then did not have the right to hold referendums on official decisions, but they loudly complained when they heard the news. After all, the Nefertiti had spent all her years in the limelight in Berlin; she was, for all practical purposes, a Berliner, thought the Berliners. The swap was called off. In 1933, Lacau placed his hopes in the new rulers; Göring and Goebbels, always looking for a way to expand their power and influence, were ready to give the bust as an enthronement present to the Egyptian King Fuad I, to secure his further sympathies for the causa fascista. But Führer Hitler, always a friend of whatever art pleased him, stepped in. He is said to have been a great fan of Nefertiti and to have seen her as a central treasure in the cultural collection of his planned supercapital, Germania – nothing "degenerate" about the lady, it seems. Hitler's dreams of the Nazi megapolis Germania soon sank into the mud of the Mark Brandenburg. Luckily the bust of Nefertiti, along with many other treasures from Berlin's collections, had already been brought to safety from the air raids and the approaching Soviet troops. The fate of the Nefertiti brought her into the zone of influence of the Allies.

What followed in 1945 is hardly surprising. The ruling powers in East Germany demanded the return of the Nefertiti, since her "home collection" was in their part of Berlin; a clear *"no way, Ivan"* came from the ruling powers in West Germany. Germany was now a little in Egypt's position in the early 20th century: cultural decisions were made by a higher authority and from abroad (rightly so, due to the lack of culture exhibited during the then very recent German past). Finally, the Metropolitan Museum in New York expressed an interest in the bust – and was criticized by Walter Farmer, one of the *Monument Men*[40] of the US army and an art protection officer for the collections in the American occupation zone. Farmer was stationed in Wiesbaden, where the Nefertiti was presented in 1946. In the Wiesbaden Manifesto, Farmer and some American colleagues protested the appropriation of works of art from historical German collections (not the stuff stolen by the Nazis). They wrote: *"We are unanimously agreed that the transportation of these works of art (...) establishes a precedent which is neither morally tenable nor trustworthy"*.

[40] Farmer was not part of the group depicted in George Clooney's film of the same name.

The responsible US officials followed the line of argument and returned numerous works of art already transferred to the USA; Farmer received the Grand Cross of Merit of the Federal Republic of Germany in 1996. However, the 1946 exhibition of Nefertiti provoked new demands for its return by Egyptian authorities. This time it was the US military government which, after examining the case, decided that the bust had come to Berlin legally and should remain in a corresponding German collection. In 1956, the Nefertiti returned to Berlin and was exhibited in Dahlem. In 1967 she found shelter in the new home of the Egyptian Collection in the eastern Stüler Building (today the exquisite Scharf-Gerstenberg Collection) in Charlottenburg. The greater part of the Egyptian collection remained in East Berlin, in the Bode Museum on the Museum Island. After German reunification, efforts already begun in East Berlin in 1986 to restore the Neues Museum, where the Nefertiti was originally presented to the public, intensified. The coveted statue is currently being exhibited in its own sumptuously decorated room. For a long time she was kept company by a bust of James Simon, the financier of the excavations; perhaps because he has now been assigned his own entrance gallery, his bust has since been banished to a corner on the ground floor. Its place has been taken by a special replica of the Nefertiti marked with Braille and touchable by all, not only the blind.

But things haven't calmed down on the Nefertiti front – the lady is a star and must remain in the headlines. For example, an internationally distributed article in the German magazine *Der Spiegel* in 2011 described a statement from the then Minister of Culture, Bernd Neumann, (*"Nefertiti is the most beautiful ambassador of Egyptian art and culture in Berlin"*) as, morally speaking, deeply cynical. At closer inspection, Neumann loosely cites the Egyptian ambassador Mohamed Al-Orabi, who in an (almost) conciliatory tone called Nefertiti the *"permanent representative of Egypt in Germany"* in 2008.

And then there is the aforementioned, recurring assertion that the bust on display is not the real Nefertiti. Well, who knows. In 2008, a Nefertiti with a swastika stamp on its base was found in the USA, which, according to authenticity theorists, is the original from Hitler's private museum. The bust exhibited in the Neues Museum would therefore be a Nazi copy (recognizable by the missing stamp).

Let us consider the copies of the Nefertiti. There are several "historical" copies in circulation – Kaiser Wilhelm II took his into exile at Haus Doorn in the Netherlands, where it can still be seen, except when it has to stand in for its well-protected original (?). And in 2015, two German artists announced they had scanned the bust of Nefertiti in a clandestine action under the eyes of the not-too-bright guards, in order not only to return it virtually to its original location 100 years after the bust had been abducted, but to make it accessible to all interested parties as a digital copy. People can download the data and then do whatever they want with it. Even print it out in a 3D printer, put it on a desk, donate it to the local village museum and feel like James Simon. But the work of the two art vigilantes, called *The Other Nefertiti* or *Nefertiti Hack*, is not without controversy. According to one critic, the liberation scan (also recorded on a clandestine video) was merely a bold deception, with the scan published rather being an existing, "commercial" digitization. I guess everything remains 100% the same in the digital world as in the "antique analogue".

The whole story somehow only makes sense if we assume (or understand) that Nefertiti simply was in the right place at the right time to become a star. Most visitors of the Nefertiti and the fantastic collections of Berlin's Museum Island (or similar institutions) will somehow question if the displayed objects from afar shouldn't be somewhere else. Some, like the German scan artists above, consider Nefertiti a stolen cultural asset, obvious proof that Germany continues to behave as a colonial power. Others see stories such as Nefertiti's journey to Berlin from a different perspective: the collection resulting from the many finds, of which the bust is just one, was one of the necessary starting points for a deeper understanding of a universal international human history that would otherwise have been difficult to develop. That said, it is of course problematic that the evaluation of cultural natural resources was left to colonial officials, even if the distribution followed an existing system promising a quantum of "justice".[41]

---

[41] I would like to offer a solution. The shop of the Neues Museum offers high-quality copies for around € 9,000 – hardly distinguishable from the original, according to the advertising. Let's get one of those and hire one of the street fraudsters still active in Berlin (for local color), cover the statues with cones, etc. The directors of the relevant museums in Cairo and Berlin may then try their luck. To make things more historically relevant, they'd have to down two bottles of red wine each. We'd end up with two stars and could still go on puzzling: where is the original (if there is one)?

1917

#Charlottenburg, Central Cemetery
Friedrichsfelde

Charlottenburg becomes Charlottengrad

In 1917 the Russian Revolution overwhelmed the giant state in the East. Many Russians, among them political opponents of the revolutionaries, capitalists and members of the upper classes, went to the West, and many to Germany. Around 300,000 are said to have settled in the Berlin area and especially in the lively neighboring city of Charlottenburg, soon nicknamed *Charlottengrad*. Among these Russians was the wealthy aristocratic family of the Nabokovs, which had German connections (the ancestry of the Nabokovs is said to include the 18th century composer Carl Gaun, a Berliner). Father Vladimir Dmitrievich Nabokov was a liberal Duma deputy who fled the new Russia after being arrested by the Bolsheviks, and died in Berlin in 1922 during an assassination attempt on a Russian minister at the Berlin Philharmonic – after having courageously tried to intervene. In the same year, his son Vladimir Vladimirovich Nabokov moved from Cambridge, where the family had him study, to Berlin. Although Nabokov, today considered one of the more influential writers of the 20th century, spoke little German throughout his life, the atmosphere of 1920s Berlin can be found in many of his stories. Like many of the Charlottengrad Russians, he left town and country in the 1930s to escape the march of the Nazis. In Berlin-Halensee, a plaque at one of the houses he inhabited while in Berlin commemorates the famous writer (Nestorstraße).

There is another good place to reflect on the impact of the Russian Revolution: the *Socialist Cemetery*, officially called the *Central Cemetery Friedrichsfelde*. Following the Spartacus Uprising in 1919, it became the final resting place of socialist victims of right-wing reactionaries. Karl Liebknecht and Rosa Luxemburg are among the people buried here. In 1926 a revolutionary monument designed by Mies van der Rohe was erected, which was later destroyed by the Nazis; these days, a smaller replica reminds visitors of the luckless structure. During the GDR years, a larger socialist memorial was set up near the entrance to the graveyard; the latter was then considered a memorial cemetery for socialist heroes.

[Socialist Monument, Friedrichsfelde.]

[Clearly labelled: The DIN-Platz.]

#DIN-Platz

The new standard

It is hard to imagine Germany, considered by some the country ruled by standards and stipulations, without the DIN (*Deutsche Industrienorm*, German Industry Standard). The idea of standardization is, of course, very old; the first national norms institute, the *Engineering Standards Committee*, was established in London in 1901 and duly played its part in the rampant success of the British economy. The story in Germany, of course, was a little more martial. WWI was in full swing when someone suggested that standardized parts would help the war effort by speeding up the production of munitions. "Nice!", said the warmongers, and founded a much-needed corresponding committee in 1917. The *Normalienausschuß für den Maschinenbau* (Standards Committee for Mechanical Engineering) published its first *Deutsche Industrienorm* long after the war, in 1928. The first standard dealt with taper pins for mechanical engineering. In the following decades, everything from nails to business letters was covered by DIN standards. The DIN 476 standard for paper formats is a particularly elegant example. It dictates an aspect ratio of 1 : v2, whereby the paper formats from A0 (1 square meter) onwards are halved in each numbered step (A1, A2, A3...).

Today the standardization is largely regulated internationally. In Europe, the *International Organization for Standardization* (ISO) in Geneva (est. 1947) does most of the work, but is still supported by the *German Institute for Standardization*, whose facade can be peeked at from the DIN-Platz on Kurfürstenstraße ...

1918-1933:

Berlin during the Weimar Republic, or:
A first stab at democracy

[The Einstein tower, Wissenschaftspark Albert Einstein, Babelsberg.]

One code to hide it all ...

Frankfurt-born Arthur Scherbius had already made a name for himself as a busy engineering developer when he registered his first patent for a new and incredibly powerful encryption machine in 1918. The mysterious character sequences of his machine would, he said, be impossible to decipher – so he called his invention ENIGMA, Greek for "riddle". It was first marketed as a device for encrypting business messages – back then you could intercept telegrams, the e-mail equivalent of those distant days, with the simplest of means, and the encryption methods commonly used at the time could be decrypted with little effort. Accordingly, those who had something to hide were happy to enlist the services of ENIGMA. In 1920 Scherbius and his business partner Ernst Richard Ritter founded a development company named after the two partners with headquarters on Schiffbauerdamm in Berlin-Mitte. Shortly thereafter, the German military developed an interest in the device, then manufactured by the *Chiffriermaschinen-Aktiengesellschaft*. The army soon became a crucial customer, and when they wanted exclusive use rights, the device disappeared from the general market. This is why the ENIGMA, although originally intended for the encryption of business messages, is primarily remembered as the cipher device of the Nazis. But Scherbius was not to not witness this diabolical development; he died in 1929 in an accident with a horse-drawn carriage.

The ENIGMA rotor machine made it possible to assign practically every letter to a different equivalent not directly linked to the allocation system of the respective neighboring letters – effectively invalidating the previously customary methods of deciphering based on the distribution of letters or groups of letters and the subsequent allocation to the standard alphabet. Scherbius was not the only one who had this ingenious idea. 1919 saw patents filed for similar apparatuses from one A. G. Damm in Sweden (used by the US army in the Second World War) and one H. Koch in Holland, followed in 1921 by a certain E. H. Hebern in the USA. But it was the Berlin-made ENIGMA that would enjoy global fame in historical pop culture – since the Nazi code, which was considered "unbreakable", was in fact poptastically cracked.

In general this achievement, which influenced the course of the Second World War, is attributed to the eccentric genius Alan Turing (and sometimes, more fairly, to him and his team of several thousand men and women); that is true, but it has a history. Even in the Weimar period, Polish intelligence was not entirely convinced of the peaceful intentions of its western neighbor. From 1928 onwards, it worked on the decoding of ENIGMA in a special unit set up by the Warsaw-based *Biuro Szyfrów*, Department BS4. While the rest of the world considered

ENIGMA "uncrackable", young mathematician Marian Rejewski used an old, commercial ENIGMA and his excellent knowledge of permutation theory to determine the cabling of the machine, one of the basic elements of the encryption process. A success that secured him a place in the annals of cryptography. Rejewski and his colleagues constructed a deciphering machine called *Bomba kryptologiczna* and were now able to decipher German military communications.[42]

In 1938, however, Nazi Germany updated the ENIGMA system; the Polish side could no longer decipher Nazi communications and was keenly aware of distinctly negative developments. They therefore decided to share all findings with relevant French and British entities; the transfer of the Polish data, including replicas and details of ENIGMA methodology, took place shortly before the Nazi German invasion of Poland. Building on this knowledge, Turing and his team constructed the *Turing Bombe* in Bletchley Park near London, which could crack messages encoded by the improved ENIGMA. From 1940 onwards it was therefore possible to decipher a large part of the secret army communications of the Nazi aggressors, which had a considerable influence on the course of the war. The role of the Poles remained unknown for a long time – the corresponding information having been declared ultra-secret by the British government in 1945.

[42] A monument in Poznan commemorates the performance of Rejewski and his team.

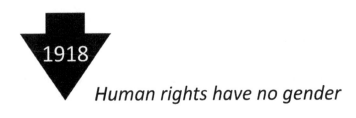

Human rights have no gender

The successive steps towards the emancipation of workers, women and the individual cannot meaningfully be assigned to specific locations. Emancipation has always been and must be a process as broad and universal as it is highly individualized. Nevertheless there were pioneers, and one of the champions of feminism in the German-speaking world is Berlin-born Marianna Adelaide Hedwig Dohm, née Schlesinger. As was customary at her time, there were only few, very restricted "official" educational opportunities available to her as a woman. Born in 1831, she first had to help run her family's household after her elementary school education. In 1853 she married Ernst Dohm, who was active in Berlin's literary and intellectual circles. In addition to giving birth to five children, she acquired literary, historical and economic knowledge on her own initiative. From the mid-1870s onwards, she advocated complete equality between women and men in publications – including, of course, equal suffrage (in the North German Confederation, to which Prussia belonged, universal suffrage for men was declared in 1864; it then applied across Germany as of the foundation of the German Reich in 1871). But her ideas went too far – not only in the opinion of many men, but also for most women.

Dohm's demand for economic independence was based, among other things, on her insistence that women should not be forced into what she called the *"prison of marriage"*. Furthermore she described the urge to have and mother children as acquired emotions; she wanted to hand over child rearing to yet-to-be created institutions. This makes this pioneer of feminism or, to be more exact, of universal equality also a forerunner of gender studies – and an unusual and optimistic utopian.[43] In 1918, shortly before her death, she witnessed the introduction of universal suffrage for all citizens, men and women, in the Weimar Republic.

Today, Hedwig Dohm is remembered at several locations in Berlin; a street was named after her, and her tomb on the old St.-Matthäus-Kirchhof received an honorary gravestone with the inscription *Die Menschenrechte haben kein Geschlecht* (Human rights have no gender).

"Women do differ in certain aspects of their character, just like men do, according to their surroundings, class and upbringing."

(Hedwig Dohm, 1876)

---

[43] A 2018 review of the film Blade Runner 2049 in the New Statesman, which critically examined gender issues in the movie, read: "*Feminism is one potential solution to this problem: removing the barriers which make women feel that motherhood is a closing of doors*". Hedwig Dohm probably turned in her grave.

The new town

When Sir Ebenezer Howard formulated the theory of the garden city in 1898 and the first garden city (Letchworth in Hertfordshire) was created as an alternative to the generally unhealthy conditions in English industrial cities, the intentions were clear and well formulated: regular people, workers and such, were to have access to a healthy lifestyle and home. The garden towns, which could be considered the first planned suburbs, were to be well connected to work centers and "central cities". It was an idea that met with keen interest in some circles in Berlin, at the time the world's largest "tenement city", in which the living conditions of the lower 90% were hardly conducive to good health.

The *Deutsche Gartenstadt-Gesellschaft* (DGG, German Garden City Society) was founded in Berlin in 1902. Its declaration of economic and social intent reads almost revolutionary today, given the way Berlin changed in recent decades (Berlin is locally known as the hip city of comparatively cheap rents hardly any Berliner can afford): *"A garden city is a planned settlement on well-developed land kept in the ownership of the community, making any speculation with the land impossible"*. In subsequent years, several such "cities" emerged throughout Germany and Berlin, where architect Bruno Taut developed the garden city of Falkenberg in Treptow-Köpenick, which was strongly oriented towards the British model. In 1919, together with colleagues such as Walter Gropius and Hans Scharoun, Taut discussed the social aspects of a *"new architecture"* within an artist group called the *Gläserne Kette* (Glass Chain). Following developments in the USA and the Netherlands, they wanted to use simple and functional approaches to develop housing that would be aesthetically pleasing, affordable and socially inclusive.

The German variant of modernity in architecture at the time, the *Neues Bauen*, was born; six such settlements have been declared a World Cultural Heritage Site by UNESCO under the telling title *Berlin Modernism Housing Estates*, thus acknowledging not only their social approach but also their significance for urban development in general at that time (strangely enough, no such honor was bestowed on the English town of Letchworth).

Four of these estates were designed by Bruno Taut: the garden city *Falkenberg*, the *Schillerpark* in Wedding, the *Hufeisensiedlung* (horseshoe settlement) in Britz, the *Weiße Stadt* (White City) in Reinickendorf and the *Wohnstadt Carl Legien* in Prenzlauer Berg. The star of these ensembles is the *Hufeisensiedlung*, which even boasts a "museum for rent" called *Tautes Heim*[44], a

---

[44] A pun on the expression *"trautes Heim"*, which roughly translates as "sweet home".

house furnished true to the original style of the 1920s. Of interest to those exploring the area surrounding the *Hufeisensiedlung* will be another estate that was built at the same time using a more "traditional" form-related language. There are gabled buildings, and occasionally you even spot a playful bay window. Legend has it that the residents of the "conservative" *Krugpfuhlsiedlung* (named after the central pond) and the "socialist" *Hufeisensiedlung* didn't get along too well. Both neighborhoods can be described as attractive and/or "*cosy*" and form an urban yin and yang of the strange German variety. A somewhat different "garden city" can be found in Berlin-Schöneberg, called *Cecilienhöfe*. This complex is far more ornamental than the ensembles developed under the direction of Bruno Taut, but perhaps for that very reason well worth a walk.

Another estate in Berlin developed by Taut and relevant to this topic even lent its name to a metro station: *Onkel Tom's Hütte* (Uncle Tom's Cabin) in Zehlendorf. The name referred to the name of a restaurant in turn named after the famous novel by Harriet Beecher Stowe. Neither the name of the settlement nor Taut's work were in any way acceptable to the Nazis, who presumably viewed this type of architecture almost as "*degenerate art*". After a disappointed Taut returned to Berlin in 1933 from communist Moscow, where he wanted to work as an architect but was unable to get through the red tape (pun intended), he was confronted with a hostile culture that had taken over his former home. Taut left Berlin again almost immediately. He then went to Japan and later to

Turkey, where he worked as a professor of architecture in Istanbul. During this time he designed the building of the Faculty of Languages, Geography and History for the University of Ankara. Taut died in 1938 and was the first (and remains the only) non-Muslim to be buried in the *Edirnekapı Martyrs' Cemetery* in Istanbul.

 **1920**

Berlin gulps up its hinterland

Berlin made the biggest population leap in its history in 1920. Some 27 neighboring communities, including the largish towns of Charlottenburg and Neukölln, were incorporated into the new *Greater Berlin*. The population doubled to 3.9 million overnight, and Berlin became the third largest city, and probably the largest poorhouse, in the world. The term *Golden Twenties* fits at most the period from 1925-1929, which was preceded by mass unemployment and the dire consequences of the world war for Germans, and followed by the international economic crisis. Berlin still continued to grow, albeit slowly: between 1920 and 1925 by roughly 150,000 inhabitants, between 1925 and 1930 by 300,000. In spite of the not-so-rosy economic prospects and the scarce space available, one officially stateless man came to town in 1928, and, unfortunately, stayed. Adolf Hitler, who had given up his Austrian nationality in 1925.

World = Nonsense!
In Berlin!!

In addition to Berlin's expansion into Greater Berlin, another major event shook the city (and the world) in 1920: the *First International Dada Fair*. Dada, founded in 1916 by artists seeking to escape the brutal insanity of WWI in Switzerland, saw itself as a resounding *"yes to the gigantic hocus-pocus of being"*. Its credo was nihilism: pragmatic, unescapable and universal nihilism. It was, some say, the only sensible reaction to the madness of the "Great War".

Once Dada came to Berlin, it evolved from an almost playful art form to something more … wicked, more offensive, larger in thought, louder, and also quite anti-artistic (see *Berlin, home of all things "Anti"*). Some older movements had already tried to raise art to the level of religion, but Dada went one step further. In Berlin, Dadameister Johannes Baader declared himself President of the Earth as well as the new Savior and proclaimed: *"We don't care about Jesus Christ!"*[45]

By the way, visitors were not always treated well at Dadaist events. After all, it's your own fault if you're

[45] Baader had already started his Jesus thing in 1914.

not an artist but audience, meaning fodder. George Grosz and John Heartfield used Dada for their all-round attack on the military and ill-conceived, nationalistic tendencies to glorify soldiers and the war itself present in German mainstream culture of the time. Heartfield is considered by many to be the inventor of the photo-montage – although the artist Hannah Höch, also part of Dada Berlin, was probably the first person to glue parts of photographs together to make a new composition.[46]

The *International Dada Fair* was held at the Burchard art gallery on *Lützowufer*, and was intended to regather all Dada forces. Luckily, elements of the Berlin audience were always prepared to play their ordained part in a juicy scandal, and showed their indignation by skillfully displaying post-Wilhelminian stiffness. Just what the Dada crew needed. Others, hopefully, had fun insulting the artists. One poster (if you could read rather small print while doing a handstand) proclaimed: "*Dada-humans prove to be truly real compared to the stinking phoniness of the family father and capitalist dying in his armchair.*" A text that could not be closer to the various West-Berlin manifestos and bar discussions of the 1980s. The fair was the highlight and end of Berlin Dada and thus of the international and cosmic Dada movement. What? OK. Dada was only really dissolved at the *Dada Congress* in Paris in 1922.

[46] Collages already existed earlier, including the insertion of "foreign materials" in paintings; but somewhere around 1920 the "re-use" of what must then have been regarded as "new media" began.

1921

[The *Tränenpalast* at the *Spreedreieck*; the former border crossing, is now a museum.]

#Wasserturm, Narva tower, Borsigturm, Ullsteinhaus

Berlin's most iconic high-rise is a no-show

High-rise buildings are great, they ooze modernity, power, wealth, they ... Wait a minute. Let's have a look at the definition. According to the German building regulations, a high-rise is a building in which the floor of at least one room used for human activities (a living room, an office, whatever) is more than 22 m above the ground. OK. Bummer. Such buildings already existed in ancient Rome (although they often collapsed), and in Bologna residential towers reached similar staggering heights in the Middle Ages. Are we really saying Berlin only followed suit in 1921?

Not quite. Berlin's oldest high-rise, according to the above definition, hails from 1877 (late enough) and is actually quite beautiful. It's the iconic *Wasserturm* (water tower) in Prenzlauer Berg, which served as a housing unit from its first days onwards. Today it is regarded a residential building no self-respecting tenant would ever abandon. Mostly, however, another building is mentioned as the first high-rise in Berlin, the *Narva Tower* in Friedrichshain. The 42-m-tower was erected around 1907 by the company Deutsche Gasglühlicht as a light bulb factory. It is currently occupied by BASF; the building has been topped by a glass cube full of offices and now reaches a height of 62 m. Still not really that impressive, even by Berlin's low standards.

The *Narva Tower* might look chic with its modern top piece, but the expressionist-style building is still dwarfed in height and style by the *Borsigturm* in Tegel. The Borsigturm, reaching 65 meters, was completed in 1924 and is also sometimes referred to as Berlin's first high-rise. A short time later, Berlin received another impressive building, the *Ullsteinhaus*, which, at 77 meters high, remained the tallest such building in Germany until the end of the 1950s.

Alas, Berlin's real high-rise icon was never built. Nevertheless, it still fascinates the collective consciousness of international (and German) architects. In 1921, Mies van der Rohe sketched a plan for a new building next to Friedrichstraße station, called the *Wabe* (honeycomb). The filigree glass house was designed to be 80 meters high. In Rohe's drawings, it rips into Berlin's classicist cityscape like a fairy-tale icebreaker: Yes, the future had arrived! But not for Rohe's high-rise. We don't know if the real building would have stood up to the super-modernist promise of the design, as it was never built. However, the ever-present Berlin nostalgia for all things 1920s led to another attempt at a realization of the iconic dream structure in 1992. The original site (Spreedreieck) was free for development, but the contract was awarded to another design. The resulting much-ridiculed building now overshadows the *Tränenpalast* (palace of tears), a former international border crossing which received its poetic name from emigrating East Germans having to say farewell forever to their loved ones at this location during the Cold War. The *Tränenpalast* is now, after a stint as a concert venue in the crazy 90s, a museum detailing aspects of German partition. Although it is quite a beautiful structure, one often wonders around the melancholic palace of tears … wouldn't Berlin be a better place with van der Rohe's daring building, and without the bloody war and history that led to the *palace of tears*? Well. Berlin is perhaps not only the city that never is, but only becomes, but also the city that never became what it could have been.

#Einsteinturm

*Ich bieg dir noch'n Regenbogen
(I'll bend one more rainbow for you)
(Rio Reiser)*

When architect Erich Mendelsohn was asked to create a purpose-built building for science, more precisely a tower telescope for observing the sun, he enthusiastically accepted. A new constellation of inspiration opened up to him; the world of relativity. The structure in *Babelsberg* was to help prove the correctness of some of Albert Einstein's predictions, who had been working in Berlin since 1914 and formulated parts of his general theory of relativity there.[47]

The building, called the *Einstein Tower*, charms terrestrial observers with its organically flowing, elegantly curved forms, predating some elements found in the sci-fi films of later years, and has been called one of the most original and important buildings of the 20th century (according to the information board next to the structure). However, it neither fulfilled its original purpose immediately (the measurement of the small redshift in the light of the sun caused by gravitational effects predicted by Einstein's theories) nor did it prove to be a robust building; after only five years, serious repairs were necessary. Still, it is and remains a building that, at least in theory, is as functional as it is fantastic – a structure whose design vocabulary remains appealing and is worth a visit to today's *Albert Einstein Science Park*.

In 1928 Mendelsohn erected another iconic building in Berlin: the *Universum cinema*, which was converted into the *Schaubühne* am *Lehniner Platz* theatre in 1981. In 1933 Mendelsohn, who came from a Jewish family, emigrated to England and from there to Palestine, where he created several well-known buildings, especially in Jerusalem. He then went to the USA, where he was involved in setting up the *German Village* in Utah – a replica of typical Berlin tenement buildings in which the effects of incendiary bombs were tested before they were used in the war.

Albert Einstein, who hailed from a Jewish-German background, left Berlin in 1932; he had accepted a job at Princeton and had planned to commute between the USA and Berlin, but the Nazis beat him to it. In that same year Einstein was one of the signatories of an urgent appeal issued by the *International Socialist*

[47] Einstein gave his first public lecture on general relativity in 1915 at the *Archenhold Observatory*, then called the *Volkssternwarte* (people's observatory) in the now aptly called *Albert Einstein Hall*; a visit to the facility in Treptower Park is definitely worthwhile – especially during a demonstration of the giant Great Refractor, or *Himmelskanone* (sky cannon), the world's largest pointable telescope, which was constructed as a technical showcase for the 15th birthday of Greater Berlin.

Battle Federation; it urged Germany's Communists and Social Democrats to join forces for the June 1932 election under the motto *"Unity against Fascism"*, in order to avert the danger of a victory of the brown shirts. Unfortunately, the left-wing forces were unable to overcome their differences. Arriving back in Europe in March 1933, Einstein handed in his German passport at the embassy in Brussels. He did not want to be a citizen of the emerging Nazi State and filed an application for voluntary expatriation, which was rejected; instead, he was "forcefully expatriated" by Nazi Germany in 1934.

Einstein became a US citizen and is today regarded as one of the greatest scientific geniuses of the 20th century. Naturally, Berlin is keen to adorn itself with memories of his time here. For Einstein, history made Germany a *"country of mass murderers"*, which he never visited again.

Dracula: The Berlin days

March 4, 1922. Berlin's cultured upper crust gathered in the glamorous *Marmorsaal* (marble hall) in the zoo, in close proximity to wild animals in cages, to experience the premiere of the first endeavor of the Prana-Film[48] production company, Murnau's *Nosferatu: A Symphony of Horror*. Anyone familiar with Bram Stoker's novel *Dracula* may have wondered how accurate the notes handed out that evening actually were. They claimed a loose connection to the classic horror novel, but the similarities between book and film were more than just vague. Yes, the title of the movie is different – but Stoker also used the term *Nosferatu*; and the name of the Prince of Darkness in the film, Count Orlok, strongly recalls the word "ordog" (a Hungarian/Turkish word for devil or shapeshifter) quoted in Stoker's work. A chance visitor of the premiere, perhaps the dark count himself, who may have envied the Berlin actor Max Schreck (the name is real) for the fame he found by impersonating him, wrote an anonymous letter to Stoker's widow, Florence Stoker-Balcome. The lady was surprised. Producer Albin Grau had not received the necessary permission from the owner of the rights to the story (Stoker-Balcome).[49]

[48] Named after the Hindu word for "life force".

[49] Some say Stoker's widow refused Grau permission to make a film based on *Dracula*, but Grau went ahead anyway; in this case, however, it would have been very foolish to openly reference the connection to the novel.

Why, one wonders. Although the "Weimar mark" was worth next to nothing in pounds, and paying higher sums in British currency was hardly possible, Albin Grau and his production company were not exactly stingy. They heavily invested in advertising, and a premiere in the Marble Palace, even in inflation-ridden Germany, was certainly not cheap. After all, they were out to challenge the top dog, UFA. Be that as it may, Florence Stoker-Balcome took *Nosferatu* to court, where a harsh decision was reached in 1925; the film was to be culled, all copies were to be handed over to Stoker's widow, to destroy them. By this time, the film had already made its exit from cinemas, since Prana-Film (some think to escape the demands of Florence Stoker-Balcome; others blame the almighty UFA, which refused to show *Nosferatu* in its well-developed cinema network) had already gone bankrupt in 1922.

Fortunately for film buffs, *Nosferatu* had crept into the wider world prior to its court date; the film survived in exile, so to speak, even if often with significantly changed intertitles. In the USA, the fictional city of Wisborg, where Count Orlok (called – well? – Count Dracula in the US version) wreaks havoc, is changed to Bremen – reason enough for some north German cineasts to wonder how different the city looked in former times (the Wisborg scenes were actually shot in Wismar).[50] The first serious restoration of the film was then undertaken in 1981.

[50] *Nosferatu* is considered an early example of films that experimented intensively with shots "on location".

Today, Nosferatu is considered a masterpiece of cinematic expressionism and the first surviving film adaptation of the *Dracula* saga.[51] No copies now exist of its precursor, the 1921 Hungarian film *Dracula halála* (Dracula's Death). One wonders if Stoker's widow had anything to do with this.

[51] A likely contribution of Murnau to the vampire myth is the option of killing Dracula with sunlight alone. In Stoker's novel you had to drive a wooden stake through a vampire's heart and cut his head off to kill him, daylight just weakened the monsters.

All hail the king of indiscretion

When Erich Salomon began taking photos around 1925, he did so not only for fun. At the time, inflation gnawed heavily at even the largest financial cushions. Salomon had already tried his hand as a stockbroker and a taxi entrepreneur, but now he found the field of activity for which he was to become world-famous: photojournalism. The discipline was not all that new, its beginnings are lost in the haze of the second half of the 19th century. Among its pioneers was the Briton John Thomson, who published a photo series detailing the life in the slums of London in 1876/77. The first newspaper photo in the German-speaking world was an illustration of a fire in Hamburg in 1842. A picture of the June uprisings of 1848 in the French publication *L'Illustration* is also often cited as the first such photo. In both cases the pictures were reproduced as engravings; a time-consuming task. And while technical innovations quickly led to the creation of illustrated weekly magazines, the cameras used to snatch the moments remained rather heavy and bulky for quite a while.

Right from the start of his career as a photographer, Salomon used a then brand new camera: the Ermanox. At the time this was the commercially available camera with the highest light output, making it possible to take usable pictures even in darker surroundings. Salomon used this option comprehensively. In addition, he was extremely inventive in hiding his camera, a knack he used to capture pictures of the celebrities of his time without them knowing it. A Brandenburg news outlet in 2018 wrote about the *"king of indiscretion"*, as he was called in diplomatic circles, that he had been *"the first to photographically prove that the exponents of political, cultural and business life, revered as demigods, are, after all, only human"*. That's true, in all the softness of the statement. Salomon was by no means a paparazzi bent on exposing his subjects, but rather came across as a friend or partner of the upper class he portrayed for the interested masses. With the same interest and care, he sometimes documented more precarious aspects of his time, like the situation of immigrants in the USA. But his real theme was the world of politics, the stars, the "establishment" ... of people who, in 1931, and hardly unwillingly, found themselves portrayed in his illustrated book *Famous contemporaries in unguarded moments*. As Salomon's habitus and style resembled that of the upper classes, he was granted access to their world in a way practically unthinkable today, since almost all media depictions of "relevant" people are now censured and/or staged. Many of Salomon's photographs can be found in the database of the German Digital Library.

During the Weimar Republic, Salomon worked mainly for the *Berliner Illustrirte Zeitung*, Europe's highest-circulation weekly at the time. On behalf of the magazine, he also became the first press photographer to take pictures within the White House in Washington.

At the beginning of the Nazi era Salomon and his family were in the Netherlands. Salomon stayed there and continued to work, while the Nazis destroyed many of his negatives. Following Germanys occupation of Holland, the Salomons tried to escape, but were captured and murdered in Auschwitz. Only Erich Salomon's eldest son Otto survived the Nazi nightmare, and discovered many of his father's photographs in Holland, hidden in jars. Otto, who by then called himself Peter Hunter, realized at that moment that he would "*not spend his life hating, but that it had to be my goal to preserve my father's work as much as possible*".

In West Germany, the first major retrospective of Erich Salomon's work took place in the mid-1950s, and in 1981 the *Berlinische Galerie* purchased the Salomon Archive. Peter Hunter, who worked as a photographer himself, later received the *Dr. Erich Salomon Prize* awarded by the *German Photographic Society*.

1927

„Die ganze Welt ist wie verhext/ Veronika, der Spargel wächst"[52] (Comedian Harmonists)

When the records of the white American vocal group *The Revelers* were released in Germany in 1926 by Electrola, a Berlin subsidiary of the British Gramophone Company with connections to the American EMI, they were successfully advertised with the imprint "Negergesang" (negro songs). *The Revelers* became famous in Germany, and in Berlin-Friedenau the vocal group *Comedian Harmonists* (six crooners from Germany, Bulgaria and Poland who took *The Revelers* as their role model) was founded in 1927 on the initiative of Harry Frommermann, a Berliner of Russian origin. The group became, after the usual troublesome beginnings, one of the most popular purveyors of entertainment in Germany and Europe at the time. Appearances of the *Harmonists* even received something like an official art status, while the members made private fortunes, recorded numerous records and appeared in films. Their repertoire consisted of versions of well-known songs by internationally renowned composers such as Cole Porter, pieces written especially for the group, and European

[52] Roughly: *"The whole wide world is out of joint/Veronica, oh, how the asparagus grows"*

folk songs. Everything went swimmingly – until the Nazis came to power.

Three of the six members of the *Comedian Harmonists* were, as the new powers-to-be noted with concern, "non-Aryans", even "Jews" – including the founder of the group, Harry Frommermann. As Joseph Goebbels announced in 1934: such individuals were prohibited from performing on German stages. To avoid all this unpleasantness, the Harmonists went on an international tour and then had their last appearance in the original line-up in Norway in 1935. The "Aryans" of the group had in the meantime received mail from the Nazi government: making music with "non-Aryans" had to stop, but there would be no objection to further performances with "desirable" colleagues. They decided to disband; the "Aryans" remained in Nazi Germany and became the *Meistersextett* (sextet of masters; naturally the English name did have to go) with three new, politically acceptable members. Despite further promising recordings, for example a cover version of *Ich wollt ich wär ein Huhn* (I wish I was a chicken), which was thematically acceptable even for the most sensitive of fascist souls, the *Meistersextett* would never again reach the dizzy heights of the Comedian Harmonists; they just didn't have the same swing.

The three "non-Aryans" had chosen Vienna as their safe haven and started an internationally oriented career as the *Comedy Harmonists*. They toured successfully through the "non-Aryan" world, but had to leave Vienna after Austria was incorporated into Nazi Germany, and eventually ended their careers around 1941; Harry Frommermann wanted to establish another incarnation of the group in New York, which failed. He then worked as Harry Frohman for the US Army as an entertainer for wounded soldiers. After many unsuccessful new beginnings, he received a lifelong pension from the West German State, since his livelihood had been destroyed by the Nuremberg race laws. He returned to Germany, where he lived in Bremen until his death in 1975.

A plaque at Stubenrauchstraße 47 in Berlin-Friedenau commemorates the foundation of the *Comedian Harmonists*.

The Man who Laughs

When, in 1940, American comic fans opened the first issue of the new *Batman* series (the mysterious avenger had appeared before in *Detective Comics* and now received his own regular publication), they encountered a face that would be formative for the future of pop culture: The *Joker*, Batman's arch-enemy, made his debut. Uh-huh. And what does that have to do with Berlin? Admittedly, this story is a tad far-fetched: The Berlin actor Conrad Veidt, still known today for his role as the romantic sleepwalker in *The Cabinet of Dr. Caligari*, was asked by Stuttgart filmmaker Paul Leni in 1927 to take on the leading role of Gwynplain for his silent film *The Man who Laughs* (an adaptation of Victor Hugo's novel of the same name). He was to portray the star of a freak show whose face was forever forced into a helpless, broad grin by a cruel doctor at the behest of an even crueler king.

The Man who Laughs is now considered a classic of the horror genre. And Veidt's appearance in the film is said to have inspired the genus of the *Joker* (or rather, there seems to be more than one source of inspiration: Bob Finger, one of Batman's inventors, is said to have suggested the movie character as a model; Jerry Robinson, also involved in the comic book, presented a playing card showing a joker). When seeing images from the film, though, you can't help but think Veidt would have made a perfect joker.

A popular star in the Weimar Republic, Veidt fled Germany in 1934; despite alleged attempts by Goebbels to win him for the fascist side, he wanted nothing to do with the Nazis and preferred to live in Britain with his Jewish wife. There, and later on in Hollywood, he appeared in a number of well-known films, e.g. as the German General Strasser in *Casablanca*.

---

[53] The creative Batman comic team liked to hint at this story; on the cover of an edition entitled *The Man Who Laughs* from 2005, a retelling of the origin of his arch-enemy, a Joker resembling Veidt's film character holds playing cards in his hands, including a classic joker. In the 2015 Batman adventure *Europe*, Berlin, still ailing from its Nazi past, is a *"bad dream it (the city) wants to wake up from"*. The Joker says *"I am a Berliner"* – but his city is Paris, where he has a devoted following he entertains in probably dazzling French.

1929

The Road to the stars

Did Hermann Oberth know that the rocket propulsion pioneer Conrad Haas lived in his native Hermannstadt/ Sibiu (then Austria-Hungary, today Romania) in the 16th century and had already engineered ideas about multi-stage engines and liquid fuel? Perhaps, perhaps not. Haas had long been forgotten by the time Oberth was born; nevertheless, something of his genius may have passed over to Oberth. His 1922 book *Die Rakete zu den Planeten-räumen* (The Rocket to the Planetary Plane) described the technology necessary for overcoming earth's gravity in detail. Along with the work of Russian scientist Konstantin Tsiolkovsky and American physicist Robert Goddard, Oberth's work is one of the cornerstones of rocket technology and is said to have inspired a young Wernher von Braun to concentrate seriously on space technology. In 1929 Oberth and von Braun worked on rocket technology in Berlin as members of the *Verein für Raumschiffahrt* (Association for Space Travel) founded in Breslau. Oberth found time to work as a consultant for Fritz Lang's sci-fi flic *Die Frau im Mond* (The Woman in the Moon). The film shot in Babelsberg added a detail to space travel that is now absolutely essential: the countdown. Oberth, together with another rocket pioneer, Rudolf Nebel, wanted to promote the film by launching the world's first liquid-fuel rocket; unfortunately the thing did not get off the ground. Lang's film also failed to achieve the hoped-for visitor numbers. But it's still worth seeing.

The *Verein für Raumschifffahrt* established the world's first rocket launch site in Tegel on a former shooting range that had become a military airship port at the turn of the century and was abandoned in the 1920s due to the provisions of the Versailles Treaty. Here, the Berlin Rocket Boys tested liquid rockets and everything else that could be fired into the sky. Portraits of the pioneers Oberth,[54] von Braun and Nebel in the main hall of Tegel Airport (officially *Flughafen Otto Lilienthal*, named after the pioneer of human flight) remind us of Tegel's role in the path to the stars.

The successful launches by the *Rocket Boys* soon attracted the military, always eager to support young, starving scientists with explosive ideas. Wernher von Braun received a contract from the Army Munitions Office and swiftly became the most important man on the rockets front. Of course, the fruits of his research were no longer to be displayed to just anyone. The public presentations of experiments, the amazement at technical possibilities and the family-friendly firing of shooting stars into the heavens over Berlin morphed into a secret military project. From 1932 onwards, Braun's experiments were

[54] The city museum of Sighişoara, Transylvania, has a section on Oberth; Oberth was stationed in Sighişoara during WWI and conducted experiments there. The place is worth a visit.

conducted at a remote military research station in Kummersdorf, Brandenburg.

"Science has no moral dimension. It's like a knife. If you give it to a surgeon and a murderer, each one will use it in their own way."

(Wernher von Braun)

After the Nazis took power, the new Wunderwaffe (miracle weapon) was given high priority; at the same time, private missile experiments were strictly forbidden – can't have non-military oiks meddling with good old fascist technology! Braun now set about developing the *Vernichtungswaffe 2* (V2, Weapon of Extermination 2) which, the Nazis imagined, would assure them a dreamlike, simple and total victory.

Shortly before the total defeat of Nazi Germany, von Braun and numerous of his employees surrendered to the American armed forces. German scientists were coveted goods at that time – spoils of war, so to speak. These scientists were brought to the USA as part of a covered enterprise called *Operation Paperclip*. In return for a pardon regarding their inglorious past, these lucky scientists were allowed to continue their research.[55]

[55] The other victorious powers of WWII had similar programs. In 1946 around 2,000 German scientists were brought to the Soviet Union as part of *Operation Osoaviakhim*, where they secretly worked for the scientific advancement of the power in the East until the end of the 1950s.

In the USA, von Braun not only developed military missiles, but soon became an important part of the Apollo program and a media star of space research. He always rejected any personal responsibility for the crimes of the Nazis, and his success seemed enough to push his problematic past into oblivion. Today, the Kummersdorf military research site has been largely forgotten, but not entirely; it is now home to a museum that also recalls von Brauns' experiments – a good distance outside Berlin, but worth a visit.

1929

The fantastic journey into the heart

The real heart (the actual "blood pump", not the romantic-virtual organ responsible, they say, for soft sonnets and the will to bring sports trophies home) long remained an inaccessible place – if it was still functioning and keeping lovers left alive. This held true until Werner Foßmann heard about experiments by French colleagues such as Claude Bernard and Auguste Chauveau on animals in which catheters had been passed through veins right into the heart. Convinced this would be useful for the treatment of humans, in 1929 he proposed a patient trial at his place of work, today's Werner-Foßmann-Hospital in Eberswalde, but the trial was rejected – his superiors fearing the tests could end fatally. The young physician tried his idea on himself and led a tube through a vein in his arm into his heart; his article *Über die Sondierung des rechten Herzens* (On the probing of the right heart chamber), which appeared shortly afterwards, was largely ignored.

The first application of the procedure involving an actual patient, who only survived the event for a short time (as Foßmann put it: "*Her chances were very poor anyway...*"), did not lead to a breakthrough. Foßmann then moved to the prestigious Charité hospital in Berlin – a position he soon lost again. The acting director probably got wind of a scandal surrounding some of Foßmann's publication (there were allegations of plagiarism) and perhaps did not agree with his somewhat daredevil approach. Foßmann's next important experiments, aimed at the use of contrast agents in the heart, took place in Eberswalde and Berlin-Neukölln. Through them, he became one of the founders of modern cardiac diagnostics. His successes brought him back to the Charité.

After the war, Werner Foßmann was judged ambivalently, not least because he had joined the Nazi party early on. Nevertheless, in 1966 he was awarded the Nobel Prize for Medicine – together with the Franco-American research team Cournand and Richards, who had developed catheterization in New York in the 1930s based on Foßmann's work. Foßmann died of heart failure in 1979.

Adolf Hitler receives German citizenship

This is certainly not the place to discuss the crimes and atrocities of the Nazis, the blindness and anti-democratic tendencies of a large part of the German population, or similar issues. But let us ask ourselves for a moment how Adolf Hitler was even able to become Chancellor of the German Reich. After all, you had to be a German citizen to be Chancellor, right?

Hitler's political ambitions were long considered harmless for one simple reason: the man could not be elected. He was Austrian by birth (and, after he had given up his Austrian citizenship in 1925, a stateless person) but with ambitions of becoming a German (something Hitler always felt he was; one of his early aims was pan-German unity). Yet, the acquisition of citizenship in the Weimar Republic wasn't all that difficult. It was sufficient to get a job in public service, i.e. to become a civil servant, and of course, such attempts were made as part of the Nazi project "Citizen Hitler". Hitler was to be appointed professor at the Weimar Art Academy, for example, or to become chief constable in Hildesburg in Thuringia. But all these advances failed because of the resistance of pre-existing structures; the respective political forces, often even coalition partners of the Nazis, quenched such forays by right of veto, mostly with reference to Hitler's conviction for treason in connection with the 1923 coup attempt. It was not until 1932, with Hitler having already run for election before, believing things would fall into place for him, that the stateless politician would be granted German citizenship. In Braunschweig, the Nazi party threatened to leave the regional coalition government, and its coalition partner was afraid of new elections (*"one can never trust the people"*; unfortunately a view that is now becoming resurgent among some parties). Hitler was appointed Reichsrat and thus a civil servant, and a German citizen.[56] A year later, he was appointed Chancellor in Berlin. A fatal mistake.

> *"It's lucky for those in power that people*
> *are not in the habit of thinking."*
>
> *(Adolf Hitler)*

The subsequent Nazi campaign against everything that was German but did not fit into their world view was brutal, thorough, and, unfortunately, successful. German Jews, dissidents, communists and homosexuals were forced to flee or were harassed, deported and murdered. So-called *"degenerate artists"*, Jehovah's

---

[56] A weird footnote in the history of German officialdom: a few days after becoming a government official, Hitler applied for paid special leave to take part in the election campaign. The application was approved. Hitler is said to have received a civil servant's salary until he became chancellor ...

Witnesses, Slavs as well as Sinti and Roma were likewise blacklisted by the brown rulers. In 1933 one of the first Nazi concentration camps was established in Oranienburg outside Berlin, initially intended only for political opponents of the brown shirts. Anarchist writer Erich Mühsam was killed there. In 1933 more than 150,000 German Jews were living in Berlin; by 1944 almost all had fled or had been deported and/or murdered. It seems incomprehensible, but this had no negative impact on the population density of Nazi Berlin; in 1942 the city, which at the time faced the prospect of being renamed Germania, reached its highest population with 4.5 million as the capital of a centrally organized terrorist state.

1933-1945:

Berlin-Germania:
That brown heart of darkness

[Detail of the monument for the Rosenstraße Miracle, Berlin-Mitte.]

#Ministry of Aviation

Albert Göring receives Austrian citizenship

If you ask who the most famous Berliners of all times are, the answer might be, depending on age and inclination of the person questioned, Friedrich the Great, Marlene Dietrich, Rammstein, Jerome Boateng, etc. Unfortunately, at least one of the internationally most famous/infamous Berliners is Hermann Göring.[57] And unfortunately, his brother Albert is known neither worldwide nor nationally.[58] Albert Göring did not agree with the power fantasies or the brutality of his brother and his cronies, and left Germany after the Nazis had seized power; in 1934, he took Austrian citizenship in the hope of escaping the brown thugs. His hope was short-lived. In 1938, Austria became part of the Nazi Empire. From then on, Albert used his position as Göring's brother to help victims of the Nazi regime, at least wherever people came into his personal sphere. He found a high-ranking position in Pilsen and is said to have helped various people flee, sometimes by forging his brother's signature.

[57] He actually hailed from the villa settlement of Friedenau (known as Friedenau because of the "peace", or victory, associated with the founding of Germany). Friedenau was founded in 1871 and incorporated into Berlin in 1920.

[58] Albert Göring's story only became known to a wider audience through a non-fiction book published by an Australian author in 2009.

After the war, Albert Göring was initially believed to be a Nazi. A Göring is a Göring, after all. When Albert insisted on his dislike for the Nazis, one of his interrogators reported "*Alber Göring's lack of subtlety is only matched by the bulk of his obese brother*".

Albert swerved two years in prison and was then released on the basis of positive statements by witnesses not suspected of being Nazi accomplices. In the time after that, the family name must have weighed heavily on him. Nevertheless, this story shows how little of the Nazis' racial or ethnic delusions held true. In memory of Albert Göring's history, just walk through Friedenau, or consider the former Ministry of Aviation of Nazi Germany at the corner of Wilhelmstraße/Leipziger Straße[59] with a probing mind; Hermann Göring once ruled there.

[59] The mural *Aufbau der Republik* (Building the Republic), completed in 1953, can be contemplated there. It shows the GDR leadership's wet dream of a content East German population and took the place of a relief with marching Nazis. On June 17, 1953, a demonstration took place in front of the building during the uprising of the discontented East German population, which was suppressed by the Soviet army.

#Funkturm (Radio Tower)

1934

Berlin is glued to the TV screen

Practically all Europeans still have first-hand-experience of the distant cave precursor of YouTube and Internet: the TV. This line of development runs strongly through Berlin, e.g. at the Krolloper, where selected citizens experienced the first broadcast of the first public television station with a regular program on April 18, 1934.

Some consider Paul Nipkov the inventor of television. That's being very generous. Even the station that bore his name used technology that was only remotely related to his. Nevertheless, the idea of the resourceful designer from Lauenburg in Pomerania (now Lebork in Poland) was ingenious. The Nipkov disk, for which he received a patent entitled *Electric Telescope* in 1885, elegantly split images into light/dark signals that, converted into electrical impulses of varying strength, made it possible to resurrect the original image on the other side by modulating a light source. Voilà.

However, nobody was too interested in Nipkov's invention at the time, which can in turn be considered a further development of the equally ingenious ideas of the Scottish watchmaker and inventor Alexander Bain

– who had developed the first fax machine in 1843. It transmitted motionless images as electronically coded light/dark dots.[60]

In the early 20th century, engineers around the world began researching signal transmission, and many used the Nipkow disk in the process. Important impulses, especially for modern electronic television (*"mechanical television"* is the name used for systems in which images are coded by mechanical means – such as the Nipkow disc) came from the USA, where Russian-born Vladimir Zorykin gave his inventions names worthy of a marketing expert, such as *Iconoscope* or *Kinescope* (both image recording tubes).

The first images broadcast by the Paul Nipkow station, on the air daily from 1935 onwards, were hardly apt to captivate an audience. The resolution was low and the voice of the respective presenter likely contributed more than just 50% to the success of a program. Since the shows were all live at first, there are no recordings of early broadcasts. However, it soon became possible to scan and broadcast movies. But ... TV sets were extremely rare things, anyway; the costs were too high. Television rooms were set up in post offices, where the interested public could gather around the rather small screens and stare into the transmitted world.

In 1936, this option was extensively used during the Berlin Olympic Games. Nazi TV provided its entire coverage area (meaning Greater Berlin) with live broadcasts of the sporting competitions used by the rulers for propaganda purposes. We'd all like to know whether, at the end of the day, the world's first television announcer said goodbye to his audience with a friendly: "*Heil Hitler, and sweet dreams*".

Talking of propaganda … It is possible that the rapid introduction of the world's first TV channel in Berlin, despite certain technical problems and initially poor resolution, had to do with Germany's desire to be first. The BBC *Television Service* went on air in November 1935 (with almost double the resolution) and thus became the second television channel in the world. The BBC is still broadcasting, making it the longest-serving of all television stations. And as far as the "first" station is concerned: yes, there are other claims there, too. As early as 1928, there was an experimental television station operated by General Electrics, W2XB, in the small town of Schenectady in the US State of New York. The history of television is simply quite international.

The Radio Tower on the exhibition grounds in Berlin-Westend is a relevant location for the history matrix surrounding the Paul Nipkow television station. Early

[60] The technology was groundbreaking, but, just like the images from the first TV show, the results were somewhat lacking in terms of quality. The first practical fax machine was developed following Bain's principles by the Italian physicist Giovanni Castelli, who, thanks to generous funding from Napoleon III, was able to set up a fax service between Paris and Lyon in 1865–10 years before the telephone.

TV signals were broadcast from here. It's also home to a high-rise restaurant with a definite aged charm worth visiting. The structure itself was the first commercially used television tower in the world. The most iconic one stands a few kilometers to the East near Alexanderplatz.[61]

[61] The Berlin television tower owes its location and form in part to the Stockholm Radio Conference, which allocated only two TV frequencies to the GDR, a state not recognized by most of its member countries in 1952. This necessitated the construction of a strong station for East Berlin (in order to avoid interference between the coverage areas of smaller stations). Today's structure then prevailed over a high-rise government building intended for the site of the demolished city castle; the spherical shape of its "head" was probably inspired by the Soviet Sputnik, at the time regarded as a symbol of the visionary performance of communism; the construction of the tower itself followed the design of the one in Stuttgart (in West Germany), the first such building made of reinforced concrete. The decision to build East Berlin's TV tower was made in 1964, and the tower was opened in 1969. It remains the tallest structure in Germany.

#Olympic stadion

Peace and harmony à la Nazi-Berlin

The decision to hold the 1936 Olympic Games in Berlin was made in 1930. After being unable to host the 1916 games due to WWI, Berlin had been allowed to reapply. In the end, there was a runoff with Barcelona, which Berlin won. Shortly after the Nazis seized power, however, efforts were made to withdraw the games from the now officially racist German state.[62] The Nazis smiled a friendly smile and made a contractual commitment to the Olympic spirit of fairness, international understanding and free access. And people believe in smiling faces.

It is well known that the 1936 Summer Olympics in Berlin should be seen as a bombastically staged propaganda show. The Nazis wanted to present Germany as a peaceful part of the civilized world. For this purpose, the *Reichssportfeld* complex was constructed – and the *Deutsche Stadion* (German Stadion), originally built for the cancelled Olympic Games of 1916, was largely demolished. The construction efforts were the first major

[62] Alternative Olympic Games were actually planned in Barcelona – the *People's Olympics* – but fell victim to the Spanish Civil War.

Nazi project to help unemployed Germans into jobs and make them believe the new rulers had their best – albeit exclusively Aryan – interests in mind. Practically at the same time, the Nazis set up a "gypsy camp" in Berlin-Marzahn, while the world was given a warm welcome. The event was a complete success; racist comments in the press and elsewhere were banned on orders from above. Visitors experienced friendly, open and effective fascist powers hard at work to make things work. Of course the "*Jews not wanted*"-posters, removed for the duration of the event, went up again a little later. Meanwhile the authorities had already prepared for the time after the summer games. In the summer of 1936, the Sachsenhausen concentration camp near Berlin became a reality.

> *"Olympic Games = A wonderful opportunity*
> *to create discord even among nations that*
> *otherwise have no friction at all."*
>
> *(G. B. Shaw, 1856-1950)*

Much later, in 1990, Berlin was to reapply as the venue for the 2000 Olympic Games. But this time, criticism was possible in Berlin. An Anti-Olympics Committee was formed, which wanted to represent the "*Berlin of protest and resistance against the capital and against Olympia 2000: the anarchists, drop-outs, punks, lesbians and gays, the alternatives, the stone throwers, fire-eaters, the grafters, the poor, the drunks, the madmen*" – and did so to great effect. The renewed Olympic application was not necessarily popular among the Berlin population. In 1993 about 20,000 people protested against the Olympic Games in Berlin. The reasons were, on the one hand, a kind of historical awareness and, on the other, that many Berliners, then a poorish but not yet so hip city, believed the money would be better invested in social projects, or in free kindergarten places. Shortly afterwards, the outcome was declared: the 2000 Olympics went to Sydney.

1937 #Ernst-Ruska-Ufer, Berlin-Adlershof

A window into a tiny, tiny, tiny world

The roots of the family tree of microscopes lie somewhere hidden in the darkness of the distant past. It is
assumed that sometime in the first half of the 17th century
a spectacles maker in the Netherlands assembled the
first microscope and thus opened the first window into
the universe of infinitely small things. Infinitely? Not so,
since light telescopes will eventually reach an absolute
limit of possible magnification, as Ernst Abbe, a partner
of the optician legend Carl Zeiss, proved towards the end
of the 19th century. This limit, known as the Abbe limit, is
around 0.2 micrometers.

Well, that is rather small, and deep down in the abyss
between things, but beyond the Abbe limit even smaller
miracles continued to lure. In the 1920s, magnetic forces
were all the scientific rage and promised a finer resolution
compared to coarse light. In 1931 somewhere in Berlin
Ernst Ruska's first *Übermikroskop* (over-microscope; we'd
call it an electron microscope today) finally stared into the
depths far behind the wavelength of visible light. And in
1937 Manfred von Ardenne was able to look yet deeper,
using the first scanning electron microscope. Now, even
the structure of molecules was no longer closed to the
human eye – at least in representation. But did Ardenne,

gazing into the world's abyss, gain a deeper understanding of the world's situation? Hm.

Ardenne also worked in research projects meant to culminate in an atomic bomb. How far the Nazi-German scientists really got on the way to the big "Bumm" is still disputed. It is well-known, though, that Ardenne was active in the Soviet nuclear program after the war, with some of his colleagues from the Berlin days. He had applied for participation in scientific cooperation with the Soviet authorities himself.

In 1949 the Soviet Union was able to detonate its first nuclear bomb. The nuclear arms race began. Ardenne is said to have believed only the much-cited "balance of terror" could prevent a nuclear war. Perhaps not without reason; plans for a nuclear war against the USSR are said to have existed in the USA during its short time as the sole nuclear power. It remains unknown whether such an operation would have agreed with the moral convictions of the then American president. In 1955 the USSR, with a little help from Ardenne, was able to set off the first "war-ready" hydrogen bomb. The world got used to a certain, constant feeling of insecurity, of threat – or safety, as the Cold War apologists would have said.

In the mid-1950s Ardenne returned to East Germany where the genius inventor was permitted to establish a private research institute (the only one in the GDR) in Dresden under his name.

The faint Big Bang

When the philosopher Democritus, around 450 years before the Christian calendar kicked in, assumed that the tangible world was *"only atoms in empty space"*, he had little idea where the ensuing *"hunt for the atom"*, for an understanding of the basic building blocks of the world, would lead. How did this story find its way to Berlin? Well. The modern image of the atom is based on findings published in 1911 by New Zealand researcher Ernest Rutherford, then professor in Manchester, England (where he worked with the aforementioned Hans Geiger): a massive, positive atomic nucleus is circled by all but massless, negative electrons. Prior to that, Rutherford taught at McGill University in Montreal. One of the members of his team there was Otto Hahn from Frankfurt am Main.

Hahn, who had specialized in finding new elements, moved to Berlin in 1906, where he met the Viennese physicist Lise Meitner; the two began a long and fruitful collaboration. In 1912 Hahn became head of the new department of radiochemistry within the *Kaiser Wilhelm Institute of Chemistry* (the building, 63 Thielallee, is now part of the *Freie Universität* and named *Hahn-Meitner-Bau*). In the mid-1930s the duo was particularly interested in the methods of the Italian Enrico Fermi, who wanted to create *"transuranics"* (elements above uranium in the numbering of the elements, no. 92) by bombarding uranium. But not all scientists were convinced of Fermi's view of the effects of the neutron bombardment. Researcher Ida Tacke, who hailed from Wesel in North Rhine-Westphalia and worked in Berlin, suggested in 1934 that bombarded uranium could disintegrate into lighter elements.

Meanwhile Hitler had come to power, and Hahn, who openly spoke out against the Nazis and the persecution of Jewish citizens, clearly understood that Meitner was in danger on account of her ancestry. For her safety, he insisted on her leaving Germany. Fritz Straßmann and Hahn continued their research; six months after Meitner's successful escape, on December 17, 1938, they found Barium, no. 56 in the periodic table, in a uranium sample they had bombarded with neutrons. This confirmed the assumption of Ida Tacke, which had previously been widely regarded as erroneous: uranium could "decay" into less heavy elements by neutron bombardment. The once seemingly solid world now started to wobble tremendously: Nuclear fission had been discovered. The nuclear age had, rather noiselessly, begun in Berlin-Dahlem's Thielallee. A chain reaction of developments was to ensue.

In February 1939 Hahn and Straßmann used the term *uranium fission* in the magazine *Die Naturwissenschaften*.

In her Swedish exile, Lise Meitner, who had been secretly informed, and her nephew Otto Frisch, published an article in the British journal *Nature* just a few days later in which they coined the term *nuclear fission*. The news spread quickly; in the same year, the French physicist Joliot-Curie (husband of Marie Curies' daughter) succeeded in repeating the experiment in Paris. It was he who then recognized the possibility of provoking a fatal nuclear chain reaction. The potential destructive power of the discovery became clear; and in the USA, researchers who had emigrated from Europe warned that Nazi Germany would not hesitate to use a nuclear weapon, which they were certainly already developing. Accordingly, nuclear research became a prime concern.

Fermi had meanwhile fled Mussolini's fascist Italy. The US government commissioned him to develop a nuclear reactor, which became reality in 1942 under the name *Chicago Pile-1*. The Nazi side did not even get that far, although a *Task Force Nuclear Physics* was set up in 1939 with the aim of exploiting nuclear fission. It is no wonder the progress of Nazi science was slow. The racist policies of the German fascists had led to many talented scientists of all backgrounds leaving the country; and even among those who remained, not everyone was in agreement with the new regime. While Otto Hahn was a co-inaugurator of the nuclear age, he played no part in the Nazi-German *"uranium program"*. Since he had spoken out against the Nazis, he must have been considered untrustworthy by the thugs in power.

Otto Hahn was interned in England in April 1945, together with some researchers who had been working on the German nuclear program. On August 6 he and his colleagues learned that an atomic bomb had been dropped on Hiroshima. President Truman had given the relevant order from Potsdam, during his stay at the Potsdam Conference. Hahn, who only eight years earlier in an attempt to discover new elements had started the chain reaction towards the nuclear age, was horrified and felt, like Einstein in the USA, as if he had opened Pandora's box and thus released relentless death into the world. Perhaps he felt even more responsible than his fellow inmates, who had actually done research for a nuclear weapon. Hahn, who then lived in West Germany until his death in 1968, became a high-profile and vocal critic of the dangers of nuclear armament.

The Royal Swedish Academy had already awarded Hahn the Nobel Prize for the discovery of the fission of heavy atomic nuclei in 1944, but he only received the accolade after the Second World War upon his released from British detention at the end of 1946. At the building in Berlin-Dahlem where the nuclear age began, a plaque commemorates the discovery. It is a place not to be missed.

"The word is the shadow of the deed."

(attributed to the philosopher Democritus)

The spirit of international friendship

On June 6, 1939, Nazi Berlin was in turmoil: Our boys are coming back! What? For a long time, no one had known the "boys" had left at all – and had, since 1936 and contrary to both all international agreements and official statements of the Hitler government, fought on the side of the fascist putschists in the Spanish civil war. A little reminder: in 1936 the centre-left electoral alliance *Frente Popular*, formed for this purpose, won the democratic elections in Spain; that was too much for the right-wingers. The military had already reached an agreement with José Sanjurjo, who stood for reactionary Spain and had dreamed of taking power in Madrid ever since a failed military coup in 1932 in Seville had landed him in Portuguese exile. The fascist-right-wing military rose up and plunged Spain into a bloody civil war. But the democratic, anarchist and communist part of Spain was by no means a harmless opponent. The putschists were thrown back, and seemed on the verge of defeat. Sanjurjo didn't have to taste the bitter moment; he died in a plane crash which, word has it, he himself was partly to blame for due to overly heavy baggage consisting of an elaborate gala uniform. Who knows? The putschists were now taken over by the arch-conservative General

Francisco Franco. In 1936 the two mighty fascist powers in Europe, Germany and Italy, decided in Berlin to actively support Franco – although both were members of the international committee for non-intervention in Spain's affairs, which had been set up in Paris in the same year. It is safe to assume the fascist regimes' sole interest was to end the, in their eyes, inappropriate and unfascist-like interference by the Soviet Union, which sided with the liberal Spanish side and supported the International Brigades via the Communist International.

Hitler's Germans were probably not yet sufficiently brought into line, or he somehow still wanted to be con-sidered the dictator of peace and benign racist progress. So it was only later that Germans heard of the *Legion Condor*[63] – a German combat force of 5,000 men who fought alongside Franco and were significantly involved in the destruction of the city of Guernica in 1937. Pablo Picasso condemned the brutal bombing at the world ex-hibition in Paris of the same year with his monumental, eponymous painting. But the world was, mostly, silent.

Thus, in 1939, Berlin celebrated the participation of Nazi Germany as a great achievement. How did they cele-brate? With *"songs, rhythms and fanfares"*. According to the German news agency, there was a lot of dancing in

[63] At least in this respect, the name of the holiday airline *Condor Flugdienst*, last owned by the British Thomas Cook Group, appears doubtful. However, the name is supposed to refer to an old Lufthansa subsidiary, *Syndicato Condor*, which was founded in Brazil back in 1927. Still: hmmmm.

the streets. The *Fehrbelliner Zeitung* called the German combat troops "*co-founders of Spain's national freedom*". The Istanbul Turkish Post reported Hitler claiming in a speech that the Anglo-French press flooded the world with lies regarding the German-Italian operation in the "*worst possible way*". Uh-huh. To celebrate fascist solidarity, part of the Wannseestraße in Berlin-Zehlendorf was renamed *Spanische Allee* (Spanish Boulevard) to foster "*friendly*" feelings between (Hitler's) Germany and (Franco's) Spain. The street still bears this name today. When an information board on the history of the street name was to be installed in 1997, Zehlendorf's CDU protested. Since 1968, a monument erected in the Volkspark Friedrichshain in East Berlin commemorates the approximately 5,000 Germans fighting on the side of the Spanish Republic as part of the *International Brigades*. An apt place to think about national friendships.

Kreuzberg: Home of the "Rechner"

Seen globally, there is no great distance between the Köpenicker Straße, where the first mass-produced aircraft was built, and the Hasenheide park, where an early version of another apparatus that strongly shapes our lives today was created in 1941. This time the monster, named *Z3*, was the world's first freely programmable computer (*Rechner*, in old German usage). The mad genius was, in this case, Konrad Zuse. It is fascinating to note that Zuse somehow managed to anticipate the story of later computer revolutionaries working in garages and other cool places in Nazi Germany; fixed on his project, he gave up his job at an aircraft factory and set up a workshop in his parents' apartment, where in 1936 he began developing the computer prototypes Z1 and Z2. After a successful demonstration, he received funding from the *Deutsche Versuchsanstalt für Luftfahrt* (German Aviation Research Institute) and was thus able to start his own company, Zuse Apparatebau, and rent production rooms conveniently located directly opposite his parents' apartment, and Zuse's parents got their living room back.

The building in Kreuzberg, where the *Z3* was born, was destroyed, along with the computer itself, during air raids in the Second World War. Today, a rather inconspicuous commemorative plaque on a rather dilapidated wall in Methfesselstraße reminds vigilant passersby of the memorable event. Since the spatiotemporal birth coordinates of the computer are rather ambivalent, thanks to their location inside the time of the Nazi era, we should mention that Zuse never joined the party, but was by no means critical of those in power. He simply withdrew into his research, into the challenges and tasks of an entrepreneur and inventor. His calculating machines, among them the S1 and S2, were used for military purposes, e.g. to make aerodynamic corrections for glide bombs. These devices used early versions of analog-to-digital converters and can thus be regarded as the world's first process-driven computers. Looking back, Zuse described himself and other inventors as *"Faustian idealists"* who fail because of adverse *"realities"* and because they need to deal with *"powers whose sense of reality is sharper and more pronounced"* than their own. As such powers he identified *"military commanders and managers"*.

Internationally, the *Z3* is rarely regarded as the world's first working computer; this title is usually attributed to the American ENIAC of 1946. There are many reasons for this. On the one hand, the *Z3* had very little influence on the later development of the computer, which took place chiefly in the USA. It was largely unknown outside expert circles; the place of the birth of the *Z3* certainly contributed to this. Furthermore, it is often argued that the Z3 used a mechanical switching relay technology, while the ENIAC was completely electronic, making it a more likely direct precursor of the transistor computer. In addition, the so-called *Turing completeness* of the *Z3* was questioned (which basically means its programming capability was too limited to be considered relevant in computer history). However: in the late 1990s the resourceful Mexican researcher Raúl Rojas, today a professor at the FU Berlin, found a way to make the *Z3 Touring complete*. The *Z3* was, by the way, not the only candidate for the title of first "real" computer whose Turing completeness was queried. Some British candidates, completed before *ENIAC*, were also criticized: the *Colossus* computers, used from 1943 onwards for deciphering Nazi military communications and whose existence was only revealed to the public in 1970. But unlike the *Z3*, the *Colossus* devices, several of which were manufactured by the *British Post Office Research Station*, worked electronically (making the first *Colossus*, the *Mark I*, the world's first programmable electronic computer). Zuse's Z series consisted of one-offs; the Turing-complete *Z4*, built in Berlin in 1945 and assembled in Göttingen, actually survived the war and remained the only functioning computer in continental Europe until the mid-1950s. From 1949 onwards it was commercialized by the Zuse KG, founded by the engineer in post-war West Germany and based in Bad Hersfeld, which leased the device to the *Swiss Federal Institute of Technology* (ETH Zurich) – making the *Z4* one of the first commercially used computers in the world.[64] The *Z4* is now in the Deutsche Museum in Munich. But the real role model for computers is, of course, the American-built *ENIAC* which, after its public presentation in 1946, inspired numerous computers in science fiction films. Modern computer technology made its breakthrough in Los Alamos in 1952 with the *MANIAC* based on the von Neumann architecture.[65]

With so many developments in such a short time frame, your head may be buzzing. But we need to take a step into the even more distant past, as all these achievements and breakthroughs are based on the genius of the *"grandfather of the computer"*: the British mathematician and inventor Charles Babbage, who died in 1871 and who first developed the concept of a programmable calculating machine, the *Analytical Engine.* His designs for mechanical calculating machines were not successfully realized during his lifetime. In 1991, however, a functional model of his *Difference Engine No. 2* was built for the *London Science Museum*, using modern production techniques. Babbage's ideas must have influenced Zuse in one way or another. The wealthy Babbage himself had the opportunity to visit Alexander von Humboldt during a European tour in 1827. He may just have left a spark of his genius back in Berlin.

[64] In 1949 a computer called BINAC was delivered in the USA by Eckert-Mauchly (inventors of ENIAC), but failed to work properly; and as early as 1948 that company let scientists in Manhattan use their "computing brain", the electromechanical hybrid computer SSEC, for free.

[65] John von Neumann (who was born János Lajos Neumann in Budapest, worked as a private lecturer in Berlin around 1930 and moved to the Institute of Advanced Studies in Princeton in 1933) developed the basis for the computer models still in use today.

„Imagination is the discovering faculty, pre-eminently. It is that which penetrates into the unseen worlds around us, into the worlds of science."

(Ada Lovelace)

Zuse was certainly also inspired by the work of one of Charles Babbage's collaborators: Augusta Ada Byron, the daughter of the poet Lord Byron and better known as Ada Lovelace (after her husband's title), is generally considered the mother of programming languages, having developed a sequence or algorithm for calculating certain numbers for Babbage's planned calculating machine.[66]

An important point, because no programmable computer can do without a programming language. This was clear to Zuse, who developed the programming language *Plankalkül* (Planning Calculus) between 1942 and 1945; the world's first "proper" programming language may therefore also hail from Kreuzberg. However, Zuse's programming language shared the fate of the one proposed by Ada Lovelace for the mechanical arithmetic brains envisaged by Charles Babbage: both

[66] Lovelace said calculating machines/computers *"can only do what we tell them to do ... they don't have the ability ... to know how to order things to perform actions ... they have no power of anticipating any ... truths"*; a disputed thought that is still very much alive in computer science, philosophy and sci-fi culture

213

are now only of historical importance. Zuse hoped his *Plankalkül* would be revived at some point, but except for some applications of merely academic significance localized in universities, to my knowledge this has not yet happened.

The time gap between the "births" of the *Z3*, *Colossus* and *ENIAC* (and possible other candidates) is short. As pretty as the idea of the computer as a "Kreuzberger" (and as dark as that of the computer as a sinister Nazi tool) may be, "the" computer was born in a temporally undefined, cultural-technical continuum spanning a period of several years.[67] It should be mentioned that in Spain the inventor Leonardo Torres Quevedo is often regarded as the *"father of the computer"*; he designed various calculating machines as early as 1900, although they were always specially designed for certain applications, i.e. not comprehensively programmable. I am not aware whether Zuse knew of Quevedo's achievements (after all, Quevedo is safely considered the inventor of the remote control), but he might have. Everything is, after all, a continuum.

[67] Zuse said: "*I am only one of the pioneers, but I have nothing against you calling me the inventor of the computer, as long as you are aware that I am not the only one; there are more than one, of course, I was just lucky my machine began operating first*".

1941

My enemy's enemy

When Subhas Chandra Bose reached Nazi Berlin in 1941, his declared goal was India's independence from the unloved British. Bose had previously been mayor of Kolkata and, for a time, chairman of the Indian National Congress party. He had openly spoken out against the colonial rulers. After India was sucked into the Second World War without any legitimation from Indian political forces, Bose was placed under house arrest in 1939. He decided to seek help from the enemy of his enemy. Such tendencies were not alien to the Nazi rulers – although, being white supremacists, they did not necessarily feel Bose to be a suitable ally, but still recognized the strategic advantages of a possible weakening of the British empire through Indian independence.

Bose's goal was to establish an Indian government-in-exile; he promised support for the Axis powers in return for guaranteeing India's independence after their victory. Bose got his assurances, campaigned among Indian-born prisoners of war for his idea, and recruited soldiers for the first incarnation of Bose's anti-colonial liberation force, the *Legion Freies Indien* (Free India Legion), which went to war alongside Nazi Germany as part of the *Wehrmacht*. Bose's meeting with Hitler in

1942, however, was in his view not very pleasant. When the dictator refused to withdraw his anti-Indian statements (as a declared fan of Britain's achievements he actually thought colonialism was quite OK), Bose felt stalled and used as part of an axis against a common enemy.

"Nationalism is inspired by the highest ideals of the human race: Satayam Shivam, Sundaram."

(Subhas Chandra Bose)

Bose soon moved on; with the support of the Nazi government he was taken in a submarine from Kiel to a rendezvous point at which he was transferred onto a Japanese sub and brought to Singapore. It was assumed the charismatic Bose, already known in India as a freedom fighter, could contribute more to the destabilization of the Allied forces at the side of the Japanese.

Back in Asia, he founded the *Indian National Army* (INA), again made up of prisoners of war, and an Indian government-in-exile called *Azad Hind* (Free India), immediately recognized by the Axis powers. Under the slogan *Jai Hind* (Glory to India), they fought at the side of the imperial Japanese forces. Towards the end of the war Bose was killed in a plane crash. But that was not

---

[68] Satayam (Truth), Shivam (Godliness), Sundaram (Beauty).

to be the end of the story. Some members of the INA were tried for treason by the British colonial government. Many Indians saw things differently; the Indian Royal Navy rebelled, and the colonial British judiciary was forced to issue a general amnesty for all members of the INA. Britain's iron grip on India had been broken. Although Bose, especially because of his connection to Nazi Germany, is controversial, he is regarded as an important pioneer of Indian independence, at least in India. In his hometown Kolkata, a small museum tells his story, and the city's airport was named after him.

1945-1989:

West-Berlin and East Berlin:
The Janus-faced city

[The *Hungerkralle* (hunger claw) in front of the former Tempelhof Airport, a monument to the Berlin Airlift.]

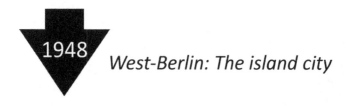

1948 West-Berlin: The island city

After the defeat of the Nazis and the conquest of Berlin by the Red Army, Berlin's population had shrunk to 3 million; those who could had fled, while many others had died in the senseless fighting. After the end of the war the remaining Berliners lived in a ruined city. But nobody felt pity for them; the suffering that had been unleashed by Nazi Germany and its capital in the name of the supremacist visions of the Nazi rulers over many Europeans and "undesirable" or dissident Germans was simply too great. In Berlin, life became a struggle for existence; in the harsh first postwar winters, many died of starvation and frostbite. Former US President Herbert C. Hoover wrote in connection with a visit to Germany in 1947: *"The great mass of the German people has reached the lowest level of food, heating and housing known in Western civilization for a hundred years"*. This was especially true for Berlin. The flow of ethnic German and other refugees from neighboring countries and lost territories such as East Prussia largely bypassed starving Berlin – West Germany was the destination of choice. There, several cities were forced to impose immigration bans on refugees.

In 1948, (West-) Berlin came to a standstill. In June the Soviet authorities declared a blockade of the districts of the city controlled by the other three occupying powers.

West-Berlin was isolated; in addition to communication channels, the electricity supply from sources located in the eastern part of town was also cut off. The Soviet government believed the opposing side would just give up the city. This was indeed discussed; West-Berlin was home to about two million people, the existing food supplies were estimated to be sufficient for 36 days. To let the blockade go on for longer would mean many would starve to death – was giving up the city the only way out of a humanitarian disaster? US military governor Lucius D. Clay advocated not giving in to the irresponsible muscle play from the East – instead, he pitched the creation of an airlift to supply the blockaded half-city, the *Luftbrücke*. The airlift became a reality and an unlikely success against all odds.

But life in West-Berlin, now an island, was still by no means easy. Mayor Ernst Reuter evoked the Berliners' will to persevere, and on May 12, 1949 the blockade was lifted; the *Luftbrücke* lasted until September of that year. A sculpture in front of the former Tempelhof Airport commemorates this story. Lucius D. Clay, the initiator of the Berlin Airlift, retired from active military service in June 1949 and was celebrated as a hero in his homeland, as well as in West-Berlin. Despite the brutal and cruel recent German history, the story of the *"Gallic village"* of West-Berlin had moved the hearts of the world. After all, it involved a greater good for which many had just fought against the Germans: freedom.

Back in the USA, Clay advocated a more symbolic project: West-Berlin was to receive a *Liberty Bell* (the original was rung to proclaim the American Declaration of Independence in 1776). He collected donations, persuaded the US government to make a contribution, and soon the bell was cast in England. Starting from the port of Bremerhaven, Clay accompanied her on a kind of triumphal procession through West Germany until the Berlin Liberty Bell was installed in the Schöneberg town hall on October 21, 1949, at the time the city hall for the whole of West Berlin. Since then it is tolled every day at noon, and on special occasions: among them the reunification of Germany on October 3, 1990 but also on September 13, 2001 in memory of the victims of the terrorist attacks on the USA two days earlier. A small exhibition in the city hall of Schöneberg commemorates this story; in front of the building, any passerby interested in history can hear the Berlin Liberty Bell ring out around lunchtime.

"Two thousand years ago, the proudest boast was civis romanus sum. Today, in the world of freedom, the proudest boast is 'Ich bin ein Berliner!'" [69]

(John F. Kennedy, 1963)

[69] *"Ich bin ein Berliner"* was not understood, as some believe, as "*I am a jam-filled doughnut*" by the citizens of Berlin; a "Berliner" is (also) a jam-filled doughnut, but that use was only common in southern Germany at the time, and there is no grammatical foolishness at work here ... The East Berlin press, by the way, did not mention his statement; Neues Deutschland wrote "*(Kennedy) raved against communism in an attempt to aid the revanchists in Bonn*", while other newspapers reported similarly and called the speech irrelevant.

"Gehste inne Stadt/Wat macht dich da satt/Ne Currywurst" [70] *(Herbert Grönemeyer)*

1949

The Berliner Currywurst (curry sausage) sort-of needs to be mentioned. It is well-known, popular and now also widely available in vegan form. It was (most likely) invented by Herta Heuwer, who ran a snack stand on Charlottenburg's Kantstraße, in 1949. Heuwer even registered a sauce as a trademark under the brand name *Chillup* (Chilli-Ketchup) in 1951.

The Currywurst quickly became a favorite amongst Berlin's meateaters in both East and West, while non-Berliners were then (and are still now) often confused by the question *"with or without"*? This refers to the intestine the sausage may or may not be enclosed in, and points to an interesting characteristic of this sausage. The original curry sausage was strictly "without", since Heuwer used another Berlin novelty: the skinless sausage. Hm? A sausage was originally a mixture of meat and spices pressed into intestines. Not such an appetizing idea? You are not alone; power theorist Otto von Bismarck was already well aware of this: *"The less people know how sausages and laws are made, the better they*

---

[70] Roughly: *"Downtown/You stay your appetite/With a Currywurst"*

223

sleep". Since everything was scarce in post-war Berlin, including intestines, the sausage "without" was invented.

Today, the Currywurst-Museum in Berlin chronicles the whole story. Curry sausages are, of course, widely available, including in the somewhat traditional *Bratpfanne* in Steglitz, where they are proud of a curry ketchup sauce recipe that remained unchanged since the 1950s. Oh, and of course there is a variation of the story that shifts the Big Bang of the Currywurst to Hamburg. But who would believe such fantastic claims?

„Wir riefen Arbeitskräfte, und es kamen Menschen." [71] *(Max Frisch)*

In West Germany, the time of the *Gastarbeiter* (guest workers) began in 1955. The Italian government had approached Chancellor Konrad Adenauer to negotiate a recruitment agreement. The West German economic miracle was underway, while unemployment was high in Italy. Although agreements with other countries such as Belgium, France and Britain already existed, there were still just too many poor in Italy. The former axis partner Germany, in its form as West Germany, was the last country to which the Italian workers were to be moved; the Italians probably wanted to forget the troublesome common past – for good reason. The German side was more than willing to accept "foreign workers". There was a shortage of labour, industry bosses called for quick solutions, and the country was not exactly too popular a destination for young workers, or even professionals ...

At first, the respective work permit was limited to one year, after which time a new one had to be applied for, or, according to the vision of both sides, the laborers would then go back "home", with cash in their pockets. Incidentally, the West German unions were able to

[71] Roughly: *"We called for a workforce and received people."*

negotiate that the rates for German workers (which were by no means luxurious) had to apply for specially recruited "foreign" workers as well. Similar recruitment agreements followed with other countries, including Spain (1960), Turkey (1961) and Yugoslavia (1968).

In contrast to previous agreements with other countries, the period of residence for Turkish migrant workers was initially strictly limited to a maximum of two years. Moreover, no right of residence for family members was granted. Both points were repealed as early as 1964, but these special provisions were discriminatory. In the years before the 1973 agreements came to an end, many immigrants settled in West-Berlin. The electronics industry in particular had a strong presence there, with AEG, Siemens and Telefunken continuing to operate plants locally. Turkish migrants became a determining factor for West-Berlin. A newspaper once did some digging: in 1961, Berlin had 281 inhabitants of Turkish background, compared with 180,000 in 2011. But – is it a success story? Yes; thanks to numerous artists, politicians, ordinary workers and entrepreneurs with Turkish roots, Germany is today more diverse and richer than it would be without them. Nevertheless, reality is often difficult, and there are a variety of views on everything. You can ponder on this while munching on a simit (sesame ring), for example.

East Berlin recruited contract workers from communist countries such as Poland, Vietnam and Cuba, partly due to the high emigration rate of its own citizens to the West. However, the length of a work permit in East Germany was strictly and consistently limited to between two and five years. No immigrant communities developed, unlike in the West. It was not until reunification that a larger number of contract workers who had come to East Berlin, mostly from Vietnam, succeeded in staying in Germany against the will of the new German government. East Berlin today has very good Vietnamese restaurants and the popular Dong Xuan Center, a kind of Vietnamese-Berlinese mall.

"Assimilation is a crime against humanity."

(Tayyip Erdogan)

#Buddhist House, Frohnau

A Vihâra for Berlin

When Asoka Weeraratna, a Buddhist and merchant from Sri Lanka, first came to Germany in the early 1950s, it was a destroyed country; the word *"kaputt"* (broken) best described the urban and mental landscape that presented itself to the visitor from faraway Asia. In a description of his impressions he noted: *"The bitter experiences of two great wars have taught them but one lesson, that all conditioned things are impermanent."* He met German Buddhists and, feeling German Buddhism and post-war Germans needed a helping hand, started a project to support his religion in Germany upon his return to his home country. He wanted to set up a *Vihâra*, a temple complex. After all, Germany, and Berlin in particular, had an unusually deep connection to both Buddhism and Sri Lanka. Seriously?

Buddhism has now become an integral part of the Berlin landscape and is a rather widespread "thing to be" among the artistically inclined and wealthier classes of society. But that Berlin, and not London or Moscow further east, is home to Europe's oldest Buddhist temple may surprise some. This story began with various German-language writers who were strongly interested in Buddhism – Schopenhauer, who sometimes called himself a *"Buddhaist"*, being the most notorious, while Leibniz had mentioned Buddhism even before (negatively). Nietzsche followed Schopenhauer's positive approach. The Russian-German great-grandmother of esotericism, Helena Blavatsky, found notable mysteries and, in her case, a somewhat questionable enlightenment in the ideas coming from the Far East.

Paul Dahlke, a doctor from East Prussia, may have first heard of Buddhism from Schopenhauer. As a wealthy, well-educated man of the world, he aimed to broaden his horizons by traveling and, one day, went to Sri Lanka (then called Ceylon), where he studied Buddhism. After eventually becoming a Buddhist and conducting numerous journeys, he wanted to establish the teachings that inspired him so in his homeland as well, and acquired a house on the island of Sylt, which he wanted to develop into a Buddhist retreat for Europeans. But the typical German hustle and bustle got in the way: Tourists were to be transported to the island by means of a railway dam connecting Sylt with the mainland[72]. Dahlke, no fool, clearly saw that Sylt would soon no longer be conducive to the deep contemplation and silence needed for Buddhist meditations. He felt a villa near peaceful Frohnau, a recently developed garden city on the northern outskirts of Berlin where he worked anyway, would be a better choice for peace and quiet.

[72] The *Hindenburgdamm*, begun in 1923, was completed in 1927.

In 1924 the "Buddhist House", today considered the oldest Buddhist temple in Europe, was completed. Dahlke is regarded as the founder of *German Buddhology*[73], an independent interpretation of Buddha's teachings.[74] After his death in 1928, the Buddhist house at first continued to function as a place of Buddhist study, but the Nazis, who felt pacifist Buddhist teachings were hardly healthy food for thought for the brutal new generations of the "*master race*" they envisaged, put an end to this. After the war, the house continued to be abandoned and started to slowly decay. More and more parts of the property surrounding it were sold – until Asoka Weeraratna arrived. His Buddhist mission raised money in Sri Lanka and acquired the house in 1957 to support German Buddhism. It features an extensive public library on Buddhism and an actively used meditation room. Today, Buddhist monks continue to live in the house, which welcomes interested visitors during the opening hours.

> *"Life is not a problem to be solved,*
> *but a reality to be experienced."*
> *(Buddhist saying)*

---

[73] Dahlke basically tried to explain Buddhism to interested people on the basis of scientific knowledge, and thought Buddhist convictions were well-aligned with scientific findings.

[74] As early as 1888 the Stuttgarter Subhadra Bhikschu, born Friederich Zimmermann, had published a *Buddhist Catechism: An Introduction to the Teachings of Buddah Gotama* to supplement the translation of Buddhist doctrine by the American Henry Olcott; Zimmermann wanted to found a Buddhist monastery as early as 1910 to spread the faith/thought in Europe, but failed due to lack of money.

"Each one of these buildings is a Diva"

1957

When, in 1874, a consortium consisting mainly of Hamburg merchants wanted to develop the area between Tiergarten and Spree, the name *Hansaviertel* seemed obvious; it is only a small mental step from Hamburg to the Hanseatic League. The plan was to create a middle-class neighborhood and make lots of money. Most of the buildings were rather magnificent, and the names of the streets (among them some well-known, dead poets from northern Germany) flattered the superiority bias of the educated classes while giving the hood a nice artistic air. Satirist Kurt Tucholsky spent part of his early youth in the area, theatre producer Max Reinhardt liked it there, artists Lovis Corinth and Käthe Kollwitz maintained studios on site, writer Else Lasker-Schüler strolled around the corners, and Albert Einstein visited the local synagogue during his time in Berlin. From 1943 onwards, the area was devastated by Allied air raids; by the end of the war, the *Hansaviertel* had practically disappeared, with most buildings resembling hollow stone teeth helplessly biting into the grey German sky. End of story?

In 1946 Hans Scharoun, an architect from Bremerhaven, was made director of the department of building and municipal housing for the first Berlin city government after the Nazi era, established by the Soviet occupation administration. Scharoun, an advocate of organic design, had essentially been commissioned to draw up a reconstruction blueprint for Berlin; he developed a *Kollektivplan* (collective plan) that envisaged the construction of a completely new city: a new beginning, amongst new constructions.

This new Berlin was to be organized in an *"organic cityscape"* along the Spree, divided into residential, industrial/commercial and administrative zones, with the residential areas each providing a home for around 5,000 residents – garden cities along the serpentine glitter of the Spree, perhaps? The plan was presented to the city's remaining population in the ruins of the city palace, but was never realized. Shortly thereafter, other plans were developed with a focus on the rapid restoration of housing and the re-development of the city's transportation infrastructure (Zehlendorf-Plan and Bonatz-Plan). Scharoun's plans were to be implemented to some extent in East Berlin; as his plan somehow reeked of Bauhaus to the rulers in the East, however, it was regarded as "bourgeois" and thus not quite the thing of the new power culture in political and ideological terms.

Scharoun became professor of urban planning at the *Technische Hochschule Berlin* (in the western part of the city). Today he is known in Berlin as the designer of the *Kulturforum* (West-Berlin's Museum Island) and especially as the ingenious architect of the *Berliner Philharmonie* and the *Staatsbibliothek*. One of his successors in the redesign of East Berlin was architect Hermann Henselmann, who was particularly important for the development of the Stalinallee (previously, and now again, Frankfurter Allee); here, monumental residential buildings were to be built for the working class – their close resemblance to imperial role models is obvious. Due to the strong ornamentation, always in contrast to "bourgeois" and modernist objectivity, the expression *Zuckerbäckerstil* (roughly, "wedding cake style"), which is often also used for Moscow's magnificent architecture, quickly became commonplace. The first such building was the *Hochhaus an der Weberwiese* in 1951, which initiated the *"national construction program for the GDR capital"* (as documented on a commemorative plaque). Today, however, some of the somewhat slick Stalinist-style buildings are again coveted residential objects; in between them are two rather modest looking, simple balconied buildings by Hans Scharoun (Karl-Marx-Allee 102/104 and 126/128) – remnants of a brief interlude in East Berlin's architectural history, lost in time, lost along the avenue. However, oscillating between objectivity, slightly monumental historicism, power architecture, quotation columns reminiscent of antiquity, socialist classicism and, later on, an interesting form of East German modernity (e.g. Kino International), the Stalinallee became East Berlin's showcase boulevard. In 1951, it received a rather monumental statue of Stalin himself – aesthetically pleasing passer-byes until the de-Stalinization in 1961, when the statue was removed and the Stalinallee was re-named Karl-Marx-Allee. But back to the new constructions of the 1950s in West Berlin. In 1957, the Senator for Construction declared the Interbau, a housing development for the International Architecture Exhibition of that year, a *"clear commitment to the architecture of the western world"*, which *"shows what we understand by (...) decent residential construction in contrast to the false splendor of the Stalinallee"*.

The first *International Building Exhibition* was held in

1901 in Darmstadt and showcased *Jugendstil* (Germany's Art Nouveau), then considered ultra-modern. Since then, the international German exhibition has been a very popular performance show for architects. In 1957 the event, now called *Interbau* for short, took place in West-Berlin. The focus was on the necessary redevelopment of the already described *Hansaviertel*, more precisely the southern *Hansaviertel*. Architects from all over the world were invited and had the opportunity to redesign a part of downtown Berlin; the result was a kind of built-up, habitable manifesto of post-war Western modernist architecture. Architects from 13 countries, including stars of the modernism such as Oscar Niemeyer from Brazil, Alvar Aalto from Finland, Le Corbusier from France and Max Taut (brother of Bruno) set to work: even the destroyed St. Ansgar Church (named after the Benedictine monk said to have founded Hamburg) was rebuilt in a (then) fascinatingly contemporary form. In the Hansa district a kind of inner-city garden city took shape, loosely following the *Charter of Athens* written in 1933, in which urban planners and architects around the central figure Le Corbusier demanded the separation of living and working areas and insisted on exploring the possibilities of modern building materials as well as green spaces galore. The new Hansaviertel was meant to boast what the architects and thinkers behind the Interbau deemed to be human surroundings, while the Stalinallee was born out of the desire to showcase and celebrate the victory of a political system and was frequently used for parades during the GDR's existence. The sheer number of trees in the *Hansaviertel* would not allow any such expression of power and military traditions – a sign of the times?

Today, the Karl-Marx-Allee seems grandiosely prehistoric,

while the *Hansaviertel* may seem a bit like a set from a very long forgotten sci-fi-film. But let's not forget West-Berlin's other architectural highlights constructed for the *Interbau*: the only *Unité d'habitation* of Le Corbusier outside of Paris (in Berlin's West End area, near the Olympic Stadium), a kind of solitary mega-garden-city with the iconic Corbusier trademarks – but, naturally, all wrong, as the famous architect saw his proportional system ruined by the regulations of social housing in Berlin; the *Kongresshalle* (originally *Benjamin-Franklin-Hall*) on John-Foster-Dulles-Allee, designed by the American architect Hugh Stubbins, which, after its sudden collapse in 1980, was reopened in 1987 for Berlin's 750th anniversary after several years of renovation (since 1989 it is home to the exhibition and event facility *Haus der Kulturen der Welt*[75]); and the *Berlin Pavilion* on Straße des 17. Juni. After many years as an exhibition space it became a Burger King outlet in the early 2000s, conveniently coinciding with Berlin's transformation into a tourist magnet. A good place to consider what architecture means to us while asking for a vegan hamburger.

[75] The first incarnation of the building, the *Kongresshalle*, was also internationally oriented, but more focused on the political and ideological exchange of ideas; John F. Kennedy gave a speech here during his historic 1963 visit to Berlin. Side note: the Krolloper, already mentioned, finally demolished in 1957 and used for a short time by the Nazis, stood practically right next to the building aimed at integrating Berlin into the international dialogue of the West.

1964 *The German Beatles rock Hamburg*

In 1964 the Beatles film *Yeah Yeah Yeah* was released in German cinemas – a major poptastic event that was reason enough for the media to search for the "*German Beatles*". The Lords from Berlin won the final competition in the beloved Star Club in Hamburg, where the Beatles honed their skills back in the day. This head-started the career of "*Germany's No. 1 Beat band*", who went on to hit German stages with hairstyles resembling Prince Valiant, bowler hats, spats and other lordly accessories. After a failed attempt with German lyrics they mainly covered English-language hits. The most famous recording of the aristocratic Berliners would be *Poor Boy* and can be found on YouTube. These days the band has a somewhat more casual look as a long-in-the-tooth rock product – donning long, grey hair and black biker pants.[76]

---

[76] Fun fact: The *Lords* were founded in 1959 – even before *The Rolling Stones*.

236

On backing vocals:
Chausseestraße

Born in Hamburg, Wolf Biermann moved to the GDR in
the early 1950s, a mere 16 years old, in the hope of a
better future in a fairer, more caring society. Biermann
became a poet and singer in the GDR, but met with skep-
ticism from the rulers of his adopted country. In West-
Berlin and West Germany, on the other hand, Biermann
became a well-known and popular songwriter whose
music and poems accompanied the struggle to make
West Germany a better, fairer, and juster country.

Biermann used devices smuggled in from West
Germany to record his first LP in his apartment on
Chausseestraße 131 – the address that also provided
the title. Since he was unable to soundproof his humble
abode, the clatter of the noisy trams outside lent the
recording an enormous directness and authenticity. In
his lyrics, Biermann was unsparing in his criticism of
Germany, the GDR, Berlin and similar difficult to suspicious entities.

During a concert tour through West Germany organized by a trade union in 1976, Biermann was denatu-
ralized in the East – and therefor unable to return to

the country he had made his home. This became a field day for the West German media; recordings of Biermann's concerts were now broadcast on TV – and could therefore also be seen in the East, even if not officially. Singer Nina Hagen, Biermann's stepdaughter, spoke out publicly against the expatriation – in the process likewise attracting the critical interest of the powers that be. She preferred to voluntarily emigrate to the West, where she became an (international) icon of the *other Germany*". Singer Bettina Wegner also protested, and suffered reprisals by the East German government; in 1983, she moved to the West – not necessarily because she preferred to live there; her life in the GDR had been made difficult to impossible for her by the local rulers.

In 2007 Wolf Biermann was awarded honorary citizenship of the city of Berlin.

1972

The genesis of the humble kebab

The history of the döner kebab is directly connected with the Turkish community in modern German society; in fact, it is often cited as a key Berlin invention. Turkish immigrant Kadir Nurman is said to have sold the very first one at his stand near West-Berlin's *Bahnhof Zoo* in 1972; kebabs (marinated, and thinly sliced meat grilled on spits) had of course been available in Turkey for a long time – albeit not wrapped in bread with salad and sauce, but presented on a plate. Istanbul might, though, have known the pleasures of wrapping dead animals in dough at an earlier time – as seemingly suggested by Prussian general Helmut von Moltke. In his 1841 recollections of his travels through the Ottoman Empire he wrote: *"A bit of kibab, or small pieces of mutton roasted on a spit and wrapped in bread dough, appeared a very good, tasty dish"*.

Anyway, the German variant of the kebab is peculiar, different; some purists criticize the typical addition of red cabbage and other, non-standard and more local ingredients, such as the omnipresent curry sauce (if requested). And its wide availability as fast food is likewise new. Nurman's idea of a *"meal in a bun"* is said to have been based on the belief that Germany is a country of workers – of people who can't sit down for extended periods of time to eat, or need to eat quickly without even sitting down. In addition, the *döner kebab* is by now a real German export hit.

Many *döner* outlets in other European countries use meat skewers produced in Germany; up to 80% of the corresponding EU market is said to be covered by slabs of *döner* meat made in Germany. However, the question of regional origin has not yet been fully clarified. Nurman has a Berlin competitor, Mehemt Aygün, who is said to have served *döner kebab* in soft bread on Kreuzberg's Kottbusser Damm as early as 1971. But what is much, much worse are claims from the distant south – Nevzat Salim is said to have offered *döner* in bread on the market square of Reutlingen in Baden-Württemberg as early as 1969. Those Swabians! Well. Berlin is, in my opinion, certainly the home of the *veggy-döner*, if nothing else. In the 1980s I often asked to have a *döner* filled with eggplant or whatever else was available back then at a corner vendor on Potsdamer Straße; and although it was not on the menu, I was always presented with a tasty meal in bread, and a smile. United we shape the future, right? For vegetarians, by the way, the array of tasty starters seen in the Turkish gastro facilities in Berlin not focused on fast food are also suitable.

#Lake Zeuthen

1972

The cowboy-crooner moves to East Berlin

How did Dean Reed from Denver, Colorado, known as the Red Elvis, come to settle in Berlin-Schmöck-witz, an idyllic and remote part of the East German capital? Reed had already enjoyed a career as a singer before he moved to Europe – although not in his home country. His ballads were particularly well received in Latin America. A practical man, he moved to Argentina, where he became a communist after witnessing the blatant poverty the unsung masses suffered there. This did not sit too well with the local rulers. Expelled from Argentina, Reed wanted to combine politics and music and went to the USSR, where, as an English journalist wrote, he became *"the man who rocked the iron curtain"*.

In 1972 the committed Marxist met a German girl, moved to East Berlin, rocked the East German charts in the 1970s and sang the praises of the vision of a social-ist world. In the 1980s, however, his popularity waned. In 1986, he was found dead by the shores of Zeuthen-see. Conspiracy theories abounded: was it the KGB, or the CIA? It was probably depression that killed the brave cowboy, whose heart was beating on the right i.e. the left side. Towards the end of his life he is said to have been increasingly critical of GDR communism – without losing his socialist convictions, though.

Besides Reed, there was a small but interesting group of Americans who studied or lived in the GDR – mostly out of a mixture of idealistic conviction and a desire for adventure. Not a bad reason.

The studio by the wall

When the Meisel brothers opened their new recording studio in the Meistersaal on Köthener Straße in 1973, practically right next to the Wall, they were already well-known figures in the music industry; since the mid-1960s they had recorded many mainly German stars, including Marianne Rosenberg. Financial support from the West-Berlin Senate and the West German government, the correspondingly high-class technology, the acoustics of the hall (which had been used by the Berlin Philharmonic before the war) and the uniquely atmospheric location with windows opening to East Berlin watchtowers soon made the studio a magnet for international stars as well.

The most famous musician who ever inhabited Berlin was certainly David Bowie, who recorded several albums and his Berlin Wall song Heroes in Berlin in the late 1970s. Later recordings of songs by Bowie, among them for the BBC version of Bertolt Brecht's play *Baal*, are less well known, but well worth a listen.

Bowie's presence in Berlin (he lived on Schöneberg's Hauptstraße, where a plaque commemorates him today, and called Berlin *"the greatest cultural extrava-ganza one could imagine"*; it is somewhat unclear what exactly he meant by this) lured other artists into the *"island city"*. Iggy Pop[77] recorded the albums *Lust for Life and The Idiot* in the Hansa Studios. Nick Cave, Nina Hagen, Udo Jürgens, U2, Falco and Depeche Mode, along with other music icons, have recorded songs for the masses in the Hansa Studios, alongside local bands, including one of Berlin's most famous music export, the *Einstürzenden Neubauten* (Collapsing New Buildings). The Meistersaal has since become an event location, while the Hansa Studios themselves are still in business.

„Sitting in the Dschungel/On Nürnberger Straße/A man lost in time/Near the KaDeWe/ Just walking the dead"

(David Bowie, Where Are We Now?, 2013)

---

[77] Pop's song *The Passenger* was, according to the singer's girlfriend at the time, a *„hymn to the Berlin S-Bahn"*. Today lyrics like *„We'll see the city's ripped backside"* are maybe not so easy to place when looking out of an S-Bahn window. By the way: shortly after leaving Berlin, Iggy Pop said in an interview: *„Berlin was special for a while. Today, there are too many artists, too many people in carrot jeans. Idiots ..."*. Well. Different times, different pants.

#AirBnBs

The profit-free share economy

In 1985 the first *Mitwohnzentrale* (MWZ, home-share agency) offered its services in West-Berlin; they arranged abodes for temporary subletting and thus facilitated the often laborious search for accommodation in newspaper listings or on bulletin boards. The idea was brilliant; by the early 1990s almost every major German city had at least one MWZ, in addition to the obligatory car-sharing agency (MFZ, Mitfahrzentrale).[78] Some eager citizens even founded MWZs and MFZs in distant countries. Should we believe the big bang of the "share economy", by many considered an offspring of the digital age, had taken place in West Berlin in an old-fashioned, analog way?

Accommodation agencies were in existence before Berlin's first MWZ, which was just another step in the professionalization and centralization that eventually led to MWZs on the Internet and to airbedandbreakfast.com, founded in California in 2008. Thanks to an internationally centralized business model, together with the cheap mobility offered by low-cost airlines,

---

[78] The car-sharing concept has a long history; the USA had clubs in the 1940, meant to save resources for the war against Nazi Germany. One of the slogans used was *"When you ride alone, you ride with Hitler"*.

a hyper-commercial *"welcome industry"* has now evolved, earning heaps of money with housing used by tourists and business travelers in sought-after (central) areas, thus displacing less affluent populations. It's a far cry from people trying to make some direly needed extra money from that unused room or being away for a while and needing someone pay the rent in order not to lose their apartment. The problem is, of course, international; in New York, renting apartments for less than 30 days is now forbidden.

All Tomorrow's Parties

Christa Päffgen, born in 1938 in Cologne into a brewing family (*Päffgen Kölsch* is now a registered EU trademark), came to Berlin with her mother during the war. Probably. Not much is really known about her early days. The tall, nordic-looking, striking woman worked as a model during her schooldays and moved to Paris in the late 1950s, where she was given her nickname (Nico), which seemed more suitable for the masses; *"Christa"* and especially *"Päffgen"* might just have sounded too German. She came to the movies by way of the glamorous world of modeling; one can see her in Fellini's *La Dolce Vita* from 1960, in which she "plays" herself as a fabulous young party girl. She then made her way to New York and into the city's high-profile recording studios, met the Rolling Stones and Andy Warhol, and eventually became the female voice of the experimental over-proto-indy-band Velvet Underground. In the meantime, she had spread some stories concerning her past, probably to cushion her difficult origin – a not uncommon tendency among Germans of the time. She was, legends had it, actually from Budapest; her father, who did not survive the war and whom she had practically never met, was Spanish or Hungarian. According to rumors not necessarily started by Nico herself (in the star-making-machine,

247

fans often do the dirty work for their idols), he died in a concentration camp.[79]

> *„Und plötzlich sieht der Himmel aus wie Blut/Und*
> *plötzlich sieht die Sonne aus wie Glut/Das lassen*
> *ˎ unsre Götter doch nicht zu"* [80]
> *(Nico, „Sagen die Gelehrten", 1970)*

Her true contribution to music and art history is likely to be found in avant-goth-folk-medieval music, a sub-genre she more or less invented with the help of John Cale. And of course in the endless tribute versions of the songs she recorded with The Velvet Underground, as well as her versions of songs by The Doors. Richard Cromlin said of her version of *The End: "She is the pure, dead marble of a ruined Acropolis, a crumbling column on the subterranean bank of Morrison's river Styx."* In addition, fans seem to be interested in her numerous affairs with famous men from the pop and film world, among them Jim Morrison, Alain Delon, Jimi Hendrix – and Iggy Pop, who, always the attentive lover, dedicated the song *Nazi Girlfriend* to her.

---

[79] Who knows, all the legends might be true; even the British Guardian wrote in a 2007 article that Nico, stylized as a *"junkie Dietrich"*, was the child of Spanish-Yugoslav parents; the same article accused her of unbridled racism and of having assaulted an African American woman. During a concert in Berlin she is said to have sung the German anthem including the banned original first verse (*"Deutschland über alles"*); which, of course, led to much booing and flying objects.

[80] Roughly: *"Suddenly the sky is just like blood/Suddenly the sun is like an ember/Our gods would not allow such things"*

Päffgen died in 1988 and is buried in Berlin in the so-called *suicide cemetery*[81] in Grunewald next to her mother. It's a good place to visit.

> *„It's not the four inch heels she wears/It's not her baby-fine blond hair/It's more the desert in her stare"*
>
> *(Iggy Pop, „Nazi Girlfriend", 1999)*

[81] The cemetery is officially called *Grunewald-Forst*; the local name comes from the fact that the bodies of suicides were sometimes washed up on the nearby Havel; for a long time Christian cemeteries refused to bury suicide victims on their grounds. At the end of the 19th century the Grunewald forest administration established a "wild" cemetery.

[Sculpture of the "proclaimer", central strip of Straße des 17. Juni, during the street festival to celebrate the fall of the wall (2019).]

#Straße des 17. Juni

The boy who cried peace

"*We need art in front of our TV studios*", proclaimed Radio Bremen's top brass in the northern city of Bremen. And, they thought, it should maybe have something to do with … media! Great. For local prestige objects, sculptor Gerhard Marcks, who had created the iconic statue of Bremen's Town Musicians in the 1950s, was the first choice. Marcks had something deep and ancient in mind for the television studios. Maybe a town crier, the archetype of the media, so to speak, the guy who tells people what's going on. Hm. Homer did write about this guy Stentor who had a voice as powerful as that of fifty man, a human TV set, running from city to city … Why not? The sculpture *Der Rufer* (the proclaimer or herald) was born.

OK; but what does all this have to do with Berlin? Well, as of May 19, 1989 (the Berlin Wall was still standing tall) a cast of the Rufer adorns the central strip of the *Straße des 17. Juni.* A statue that was meant to symbolize the way media works thus became a symbol of peace and freedom at the hands of the visionary Berlin city planners. Well. Is it just a coincidence that visiting President Ronald Reagan had famously cried *"Mr. Gorbachev, tear down this wall"* in 1987 very near the location of said statue?

1989-?:

Berlin unified:
Too sexy for itself?

[The *"robber wheel"* in front of the Volksbühne, view of the television tower along Rosa-Luxemburg-Straße.]

1989

Eeny, meeny, miney, moe –
East Berlin gets a colorful wall, too

Back in the old, old days during a feast of King Belshazzar, the draconian ruler of the Old Testament had incomprehensible signs appear on a wall which only the prophet Daniel knew how to interpret. *"Mene Mene Tekel"*, read good Daniel, which, said the prophet, meant something like "weighed and found too light", i. e. the disrespectful king was to die at the hand of the universal ruler and cryptic author, who was setting a trend. Graffiti were to become a real hit spanning the ages; even old Bismarck immortalized himself, sitting in jail, with graffiti incomprehensible to the henchmen of power of his day. Modern times, of course, moved the whole thing up a notch – and invented the Berlin Wall: a gigantic canvas for the doodles, scribbles and messages of the somewhat creatively-minded, politically-inclined or simply intoxicated. At least on the western side.[82]

---

[82] The modern movement of mural paintings, the *muralismo*, is often traced back to the Mexican artist Diego Rivera and assigned to the left spectrum; advertising pictures on walls have been around for some time. In the GDR murals were used as an optimistic (and often false) "mirror" of the new Germany, one example being *Aufbau der Republik* at the corner Leipziger Straße/Wilhelmstraße. It had replaced a martial relief featuring heroic Nazi soldiers. In West Germany works related to the muralismo found their way to Bremen in the 1970s; in 1975 Ben Wagin's *Weltbaum*, located on a firewall opposite the Tiergarten S-Bahn station, was the first such painting to impress at least one new Berliner of the 1980s. An office building is currently being erected in front of the *Weltbaum*. In the new Berlin nothing survives a *"top location for creativity"* (advertising text of the developer, whose goal is to help professionals realize "great visions"), but the painting has by now been recreated on a wall in the Lehrter Straße, Moabit.

The inside facing wall of the GDR capital was more of a naked concrete work slightly reminiscent of a brutalist monochrome installation piece. The eastern part of the city, perhaps proof of the proverbial sense of irony the general history of mankind is said to indulge in, only got a colorful stretch of concrete after the fall of the Wall. But, while western expressions of freedom vanished, the graffities in the East were to remain. Why?

In 1989, mere weeks after the fall of the Wall, artists' associations from both parts of the city discussed a pan-German art project, and even the outgoing GDR government liked the idea of having a long strip of the *"anti-fascist protection wall"* designed by creative people recognized as such by the relevant associations and artists' committees (the often anonymous and not always superartistic artists of the west side receded into history, their works are now only blobs of color on the various pieces of the wall in private collections/drawers). The *East Side Gallery* was born and almost immediately declared a protected institution. Someone even started efforts to put it on UNESCOs World Heritage List. Nevertheless, during the existence of the painted eastern wall it often so happened that hapless anarchists would scribble and doodle away on top of the art on the cement canvas, thinking it was still a free-for-all-wall. In early 2000 the *East Side Gallery* was to be "renovated" for the first time – which led to problems with some of the artists who felt they should have been asked or protested the low "re-promotion money". There are, incidentally, always some tourists who think the tourist-friendly-named *East Side Gallery* is covered with original works preserved from the time of the Cold War. Do let them know.

The preservation of the *East Side Gallery*, a section of which was to give way to capitalist reconstruction, is important to many. In 2013, even the American singer and sometime actor David *the Hof* Hasselhoff found his way to the Yaam Club to boldly stand in the way of anti-artistic construction efforts. After all, according to certain people, the East German population simply took his 1989 song *I've been looking for Freedom* and Ronald Reagan's 1987 statement, *"Mr. Gorbachev, tear down this wall"* too seriously. Reagan mentioned in his speech that he had read *"This wall will fall, for dreams become reality"* somewhere on the wall; the writing would have been, however, on the western side of the wall, which was removed along with the text that inspired Reagan.[83]

[83] Reagan's speech against the backdrop of the "walled in" Brandenburg Gate impressed some of the people present – among them Helmut Kohl, who stood close to the then US president and perhaps already chipped away at the wall in his mind, as well as the East German bureaucrat Günther Schabowski, who triggered the actual fall of the Wall a little more than two years later by using imprecise expressions, and the inhabitants of the Kreuzberg 36 district, who were confined to their neighborhood for the sake of peace, as they were generally considered anti-American and disruptive

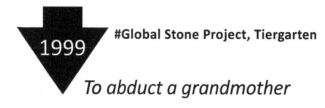

#Global Stone Project, Tiergarten

1999

To abduct a grandmother

When a curious-looking red stone appeared in Berlin's Tiergarten near the Brandenburg Gate in 1999, it became a popular meeting place for locals; some saw it as a distant relative of The Beatles' Yellow Submarine, others as the nose of Cyrano de Bergerac. At first, only a very few suspected it to actually be the rebellious, abducted grandmother of a native Latin American tribe turned to stone. But first things first.

The *Global Stone Project*, whose first materialization was said splendid red stone, is something like the life's work of the sailor and artist Kraker von Schwarzenfeld. At some point during his travels Schwarzenfeld, marked by the terrible experience of World War II, had the idea of gathering stones from all continents of the world in Berlin and connecting them, philosophically and spiritually, with sister stones on their native continents.[84] These stones were to symbolize global unity along with the *"five steps to peace"* according to Schwarzenfeld: Awakening > Hope > Forgiveness > Love > Peace. In the meantime the project has been completed; the ten

---

[84] Somehow a refreshingly old-fashioned, optimistic way of networking the world: an activity otherwise often claimed as a unique selling point by international web apologists, internet artists, Facebook creators, etc.

stones are in their respective places, the energy lines connect the various continents with the Tiergarten, and Berlin is somehow (of course) the center of the world; the path to peace is open ... if it weren't for the story of the first red stone, the *Stone of Love* hailing from the Americas.

> *„El pueblo Pemón alega que los alemanes no están en posición de hacer exigencias, pues la extracción de la piedra violentó sus derechos culturales y de credo. No obstante, señalan que no se niegan a entregar una piedra de iguales dimensiones pero sin ningún significado cultural para ellos." [85]*
>
> *(Portals entornointelligente.com, „La Piedra Kueka, mito o realidad en Venezuela")*

Shortly after the stone of love was installed in Berlin, voices from Venezuela came forward telling a different story. The stone was kidnapped and brought to Germany against the wishes of the Pemón, for whom it is part of their spiritual worldview as the *Piedra Kueka*. The stone, according to an old legend of the Pemón, had once been a pretty girl who rebelled against the dictates of a jealous god who only allowed marriages inside the tribe by falling in love with a pretty boy from another tribe.

---

[85] Roughly: *"The Pemón point out that the Germans have no right to make any demands, since the theft of the stone violates the cultural and spiritual rights of the Pemón. Still, they would be willing to hand over a stone of equal dimensions, but without cultural significance to them."*

They got married. When the xenophobic god got wind of this, he did what gods do and condemned the rebellious lovers. More precisely: he granted them eternal, insurmountable and thus agonizing closeness by transforming them into stones. These two stones are now considered the grandmother and grandfather of the Pemón (in whose language *Kueka* means "grandmother"). Since Schwarzenfeld's cruel abduction of the grandmother, destined to be the heart of love in the center of peace, the matter has occupied courts, journalists, politicians, activists and other professionals, overshadowing the otherwise beautiful and somehow optimistic project in the Tiergarten.

"Well, Germans shouldn't have visions, we know what that leads to", some may murmur. Schwarzenberg says he never wanted to rob a granny. Was the whole thing just another horrible tragedy, involving a hapless do-gooder hellbent on peace? Let's see. The stone came to Berlin with a signed, official deed of donation, although the legal validity of the signature is in question. But there are also doubts regarding the justification of the claims of return. Schwarzenfeld has now published his memories of the selection process and the transportation of the stone on the *Global Stone Project* website. Since, according to his own statements, he had frequent contact with Pemón, who never mentioned possible spirits inside the stone, one statement stands against another. The experts are also divided. Schwarzenfeld proved to be open-minded and offered the Venezuelan government, which had given him the stone as a gesture, an exchange

for another (hopefully non-spiritual) stone – but stated he didn't have the money to pay for the transportation (the *Global Stone Project* is privately financed and not a project of the German government).

The artistic-utopian idea that gave birth to a beautiful, international place in Berlin has meanwhile become a point of contention.[86] Meanwhile, of course, the Venezuelan government has changed. The Caldera government, in power until 1998, was interested in good relations with Germany, while the subsequent Chavez regime stylized itself more as a strong and proactive protector of native rights. Schwarzenfeld may have simply come between the mills of big time politics. But perhaps the story of the racist god is true (it is propagated in various YouTube-videos, but just as often questioned), and after the god's righteous anger increased over the millennia, he finally decided the two love stones were just too close together for comfort; where they able to whisper sweet nothings

---

[86] And a sore point for the artist; on his website (globalstone.de), he attempts to defend his actions: *"14 years ago it was claimed the stone was a jasper, a semi-precious stone. It's a sandstone. It was claimed the stone was stolen. No. It was a documented gift by the Venezuelan people to the German people as a part of the Global Stone Project I had started. Ten years later the stone was declared sacred. The stone was selected by the representative of the nature conservation authority and his five indigenous employees among many such stones. If this stone had had meaning in their culture, the people living near the site would have chosen another stone or prevented this stone from being given away. The claim of the sacred stone is a purposeful lie."* A documentary film detailing the fight to get the stone back was made in 2017: *Kueka, cuando las piedras hablan (Kueka – When stones speak)*. At least in the trailer, Schwarzenfeld is referred to as a "stone collector".

to each other? Did empathic birds relay messages? Or did the mighty free, grandmotherly spirit of *Kueka* want to see something else for a change and bring love to the world as the central stone of a global magic project, thus drawing Schwarzenfeld towards her? Who knows.

However, if the stone is returned – which is most likely the only solution out of this jumble of accusations and confirmations – it will hardly be recognized by the Pemón, the grumbling god and the enchanted grandfather stone that was left behind; in photos taken during the transport it resembles a large grey monster somewhat reminiscent of a whale. In the meantime, however, the surfaces of the Stone of Love and the other global stones have been polished and inscribed. Kueka is now really beautiful, to my European eyes, and very different from what she once looked like. As Schwarzenfeld explains: the stones are meant to reflect light back to the sun at the summer solstice, which somehow spiritually connects them to their sister stones on the other continents, in a mystical and optimistic way. The American Stone of Love is located in a park in Caracas (it is not the Grandfather Stone; that one is likely still in the Canaima National Park in Venezuela). An article on the Asian *Stone of Forgiveness* in Bhutan, published on the Global Stone website, talks of prayer sessions for peace next to the stone; one participant was reported as saying: "*It is nice to be part of something good*".

„Wer zugibt, dass er Unrecht hat, beweist, dass er gescheiter geworden ist"[87] (Marlene Dietrich)

2002

Marie Magdalene Dietrich, born in 1901 in Berlin-Schöneberg, not far from the Gasometer (built in1908), felt the attraction of the stage at an early age. After first roles in Berlin theaters she made a number of appearances in silent movies, but her big break came with the second German "talky", *The Blue Angel*. The film made her a world star in 1930, not least because of her interpretation of the song *Ich bin von Kopf bis Fuß auf Liebe eingestellt* (Falling in Love Again) written by Friedrich Hollander, which practically cemented her early typification as a *femme fatal*. Soon afterwards, she worked with Austrian director Josef von Sternberg in Hollywood. Being an intelligent woman, she refused the advances of the Nazis who, naturally, liked to count celebrities among their supporters. Instead she took American citizenship and sang for US troops. Some Germans and Berliners have always been proud of Marlene Dietrich for this very reason; others were (and maybe are) not.

In 1962 Marlene Dietrich became a link between the American and German peace movements with the German version of the song *Where have all the flowers*

[87] Roughly: *"Admitting mistakes demonstrates an increase in intelligence"*.

gone by Pete Seegers, *Sag mir, wo die Blumen sind*. When she sang the German version of the song on a concert tour through Israel, she broke the previously unofficial taboo of singing German on Israeli stages.

Marlene Dietrich was and is also regarded as an influential style icon. She often wore men's clothes, playing with the androgyny later celebrated by David Bowie and others.

When Marlene Dietrich died in 1992 and was to be buried in Berlin, honorary citizenship for the city's famous daughter came under discussion – but the idea was put on ice. Were the upright city officials afraid of the conservative, patriotic feelings of their fellow Germans, despite the many Berliners and non-Berliners who visited the grave to pay their last respects, despite the mountain of suitcases given to the actress as a final escort, despite the fact that she was an icon for the "good" Germany? [88]

In 2002, Marlene Dietrich was declared an honorary citizen of Berlin. Better late than never.

[88] *Ich hab noch einen Koffer in Berlin* (I'm keeping a suitcase in Berlin) was a popular song from the 1950s, recorded by Marlene Dietrich, and written by Aldo Pinelli (who hailed from Italy and became famous in Germany in the 1930s) and the Munich composer Ralph Maria Siegel.

[The Spreebogen, seen from the roof of the Futurium.]

#Federal Chancellery, Spreebogen, Straße des 17. Juni

The world marvels at Berlin and Germany

In 2005 some still thought of Germany as the *"sick man of Europe"*. National unemployment was around 12%, a high figure for post-war Germany and, according to local lore, artificially maintained by specialized state programs and what some would call "tricks" (German powers-that-be do everything for their low unemployment figures, as they are considered the main sign of a successful government). It was an election year. The left-wing (SPD) Schröder government, which had been trying to fight the *"German crisis"* with often unpopular reforms for some time, had a tight show-off with the CDU. And lost by a narrow margin. The chancellor's office in Berlin went to Angela Merkel, later the leader of a grand coalition.

Born in Hamburg, Angela Merkel moved with her family to the GDR only a few weeks after her birth. She grew up, married, moved to East Berlin, got divorced, but kept her husband's name, and then wrote her dissertation in 1986 with the enticing title: *Untersuchung des Mechanismus von Zerfallreaktionen mit einfachem Bindungsbruch und Berechnung ihrer Geschwindigkeitskonstanten aufgrund quantenchemischer und statistischer Methoden* (Investigation of the Mechanism of Decay Reactions with a Simple Breach of Bond and Calculation of their Velocity Constants based on Quantum Chemical and Statistical Methods). The scientist remained politically inconspicuous. Until the fall of the Wall. Merkel was active in an East German party called the *Demokratischer Aufstand* and received a post in the first (and last) freely elected government of the GDR. Once the *Aufstand* had merged with the CDU, Merkel quickly took top positions in the party and in the government of a newly united Germany. Still, the CDU's narrow victory in 2005 and Merkel's chancellorship came as a surprise to many. The left spectrum feared a shift to the right. International commentators really hadn't a clue about what to think of her. Was she a new Thatcher? Or just another interlude? Some even questioned her aptness due to mistakes she made during pre-election interviews.

During her many years as head of government, Angela Merkel underwent extreme changes, at least in the perception of non-establishment people at home and abroad. Her position during the financial crisis met with broad and sometimes violent rejection in southern European countries severely affected by said crisis. Unforgotten are the images of protest posters equating Merkel and Germany with the Nazis. Some even portrayed Merkel as a "new Hitler". Many seemed certain that the crisis had a clear culprit and profiteer in distant Berlin. As if to validate such opinions, the German economy slowly began to recover. Later, Merkel came to be seen by many as a guarantor of stability and human politics, especially because of her attitude during the refugee crisis of 2015. Ironically, it is precisely this attitude that has earned her international acclaim while in Germany, groups with a strong right-wing orientation such as the AfD were now portraying Merkel as a *"traitor to the people"* could feed on emerging fears of marginalization due to *"foreign infiltration"*. Merkel herself remained calm about all this, at least in front of the cameras. She has long widely been considered the *"most powerful woman in the world"*. Besides this somewhat peculiar distinction, she also came second in the Forbes business magazine's ranking of the world's most powerful people in 2012, after the back-then US President Obama.

Merkel's workplace, the Federal Chancellery on the Spreebogen, is considered the largest government building in the world. Built during Chancellor Kohl's time in office, it was given the meanwhile almost forgotten nickname *Kohlosseum*. The Spreebogen is a piece of land roughly denominated by an imaginary line stretching from the Reichstag, the seat of German democracy, to the Federal Chancellery and a "bow" in the Spree. It is distinguished by two missing buildings one might want to imagine when visiting the site (a suitable vantage point to view the Spreebogen is the roof of the *Futurium*, a futuristic science museum on the other side of the Spree). One of them is the gigantic *Ruhmeshalle* (Hall of Fame) which was planned for the Nazi "world capital" *Germania*[89] roughly between today's Federal Chancellery and the main railway station. Even the Spree was to be diverted to create space for the massive structure. The top of the dome, projected to reach over 300 m, was to be dominated by a swastika. The power-drunken architects of this monster wanted to preserve the Reichstag as a mere dwarf nearby, probably to show how miserly democracy was compared to the will of the Nazi people. This did not happen, fortunately.

The second missing building is the *Bürgerforum* (Citizen's Forum). If you imagine the place from above, or consider it from the roof of the *Futurium*, the Federal Chancellery and the buildings to its east form a broken line or belt, the *Band des Bundes* (Federal Belt). This structure would have been completed by

[89] A suitable place to reflect upon the *Germania* project is the *Schwerbelastungskörper* (heavy load-bearing body) in the Tempelhof district on Loewenhardt Dam. It was built to determine whether the local soil could carry the planned triumphal buildings of the gigantic north-south axis at a.

the *Bürgerforum*. The Band was intended to symbolize the unity between East and West Germany by connecting the two previously separate parts of the cities. The *Bürgerforum* was planned at the now empty location between the Chancellery and the *Paul-Löbe-Haus*, the first building towards the East. As a central component, it was to be open to the public and could have symbolized the actual power of the people over the politicians. Perhaps it would also have been perceived as a kind of *Palast der Republik* (Palace of the Republic) of the united Germany – a cultural and entertainment building with some political functions. In the meantime, the plans for the *Bürgerforum* have been abandoned. Safety concerns and the needs of road traffic took precedence over the symbolism of democracy.

Despite the lack of a *Bürgerforum*, the Berlin government district is worth a visit, especially the areas directly on the Spree. Here, Berlin can certainly look like a city of the future. Even or maybe because one never forgets the virtual shadow of the *Ruhmeshalle*.

One year after Angela Merkel moved into the Federal Chancellery, Germany hosted the 2006 Football World Cup. The World Cup finally made Berlin an international destination for mass tourism. Visitors came from everywhere, and there was extensive coverage, bringing modern Germany to millions of international TV screens. Instead of witnessing a bunch of grumpy, xenophobic Germans, viewers and visitors saw a party-and-football-nation that generously cheered every team on the fan mile along the Straße des 17. Juni and at the plethora of public viewing opportunities (almost every bar and restaurant in town). Also, the Germans seemed to (mostly) easily accept the fact that the trophy went to Italy.

Many Germans were a little worried about the many German flags that suddenly hung out of windows or were painted on young cheeks. But by consensus, the new German patriotism was seen as a "soft" version of this sad state of mind in historical and international comparison. It was the big day of soccer as a "racism-free" patriotism, formerly only deemed possible in hotter countries. Some were quite astonished by Angela Merkel, who liked to watch the games of the national team and gaily cheered at goals, mostly surrounded by rather dull looking (male) celebrities and politicians.

But the World Cup was not just sunshine and roses, even though some media professionals tried to declare Germany a *"summer fairy tale"* in 2006. In 2015, the German weekly Der Spiegel reported possible irregularities in the process that led to the World Cup being held in Germany. Did the German Football Association actually buy Germany's "fairy tale"?

Berlin's popularity as a tourist destination has risen enormously since 2006. From about 7 million visitors per year at that time to almost 14 million in 2018, of which about half were visitors from abroad. In Europe, only Paris and London attract more people.

A walk down the Straße des 17. Juni from the Brandenburg Gate to the *Siegessäule* (Victory Column) is a good chance to think of this history. Along the street there are many references to Berlin's difficult past, from the *Quadriga to the Soviet Memorial.* In addition, the fan miles for world championships are set up here, and for a long time the *Siegessäule* was the central DJ stand for the *Love Parade*, which had earlier established Berlin as an international mass discotheque (albeit as one without the restrictive door policy of current mass clubs). Perhaps more importantly, a visitor from the USA wrote history here in 2008. Barack Obama, then a presidential candidate, gave an optimistic speech at the *Siegessäule* that was followed worldwide. Native and new or newish Berliners came in large numbers to hear the message of the future US president, whose theme was that history could go from bad to better, from dictatorship to freedom.

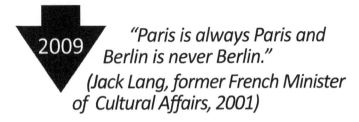

2009 *"Paris is always Paris and Berlin is never Berlin."*
(Jack Lang, former French Minister of Cultural Affairs, 2001)

The Berliners may not have believed their eyes, but there it was, in black and white, in the newspaper – in all the newspapers: in 2009 Berlin received the *Premio Principe de Asturias de la Concordia* for the peaceful revolution of 1989, as an example of a city in transition, a cosmopolitan and tolerant metropolis striving to maintain its open character (this is not a direct quotation, but more or less how the then mayor of Berlin, Klaus Wowereit, put it). Nice, and only maybe deserved. But perhaps some Berliners were already somewhat blasé due to the city's international reputation as a place of mucho cool and peace – it is often said (see previous chapter) that the 2006 soccer World Cup with the final in Berlin was the decisive factor behind the current attraction of the city and its improved global image.[90]

---

[90] Was it just Berlin's reputation that improved, or also that of Germany and the Germans; after all, the saying *"Berlin is not Germany"* is popular among Berliners and visitors. Hm. I personally believe Berlin to be the most "German" city in Germany – not only because it is the seat of government, but because the North, South, East, West and Central Germans come together here and coexist peacefully with other Berliners, and because Berlin lived the German partition and the later unification in such an intense way.

2017

Rosa Parks' house is on the move

When Rosa Louise Parks refused to vacate her bus seat for a white passenger in Montgomery, Alabama on December 1, 1955, she was arrested – and made history. While Parks was on trial, civil rights activists swiftly organized a boycott of the city's bus system, led by the newly formed *Montgomery Improvement Society*, whose members included a young Martin Luther King, Jr., amongst others. In February 1956 Fred Grey filed a lawsuit (Browder vs. Gayle) with the relevant United States District Court, covering several cases of African American citizens who refused to give up their seats in the regional, racially segregated bus system. The eponymously named case of Aurelia Browder came first in alphabetical order and had occurred eight months before Rosa Parks' refusal; W. Gayle was then mayor of Montgomery.

On December 20, 1956 the U.S. Supreme Court declared racial segregation in Alabama's buses unconstitutional. The civil rights movement took off and made the United States a fairer, better and more attractive place. In 1983 Rosa Parks was inducted into the *Michigan Women's Hall of Fame*; later, a statue of Parks was placed in the US Capitol, Detroit's 12th Street was renamed Rosa Parks Boulevard, and in Montgomery a Rosa Parks Museum was inaugurated in the year 2000. The bus in which Parks refused to surrender her seat is now on display in the Henry Ford Museum in Dearborn/Detroit. In 2012 President Obama took a seat there. A tough fight, a happy ending?

Rosa Parks left Montgomery in 1957; her bold deed had earned her hatred and death threats. She moved to her brother in Detroit in the more tolerant north of the USA and into an overcrowded house on South Deacon Street – not one of the better areas of the city, but still a place far away from the racist South, but ... Detroit did not really fulfill Parks' hopes: Later on, she said in an interview it wasn't much better than Montgomery in terms of equality. In 1994 she was beaten during a robbery in her house[91]; the burglar was African American, the public appalled. The criminal was soon arrested by local residents and handed over to the police. Rosa Parks did, rightly and optimistically so, not agree with the then widespread opinion (among the white ruling classes) that young African Americans were a lost generation. Instead, she condemned the living conditions that pushed people to become callous and hard, and, in the end, to inflict suffering on others. Rosa Parks died in 2005.

> *"I would like to be known as a person who is concerned about freedom and equality and justice and prosperity for all people."*
> *(Rosa Parks)*

In 2017 the house in which Rosa Parks lived with her brother in Detroit in the late 1950s was threatened with demolition, and Parks' niece turned to a US artist who took care of the building and brought it to Wedding, Berlin (the city that *"claims with some insistence to be a suburb of freedom"*, as the *Berliner Zeitung* wrote in an article on the house trip in April 2017, not without irony).

---

[91] It wasn't the same house; Parks moved several times in Detroit.

The undertaking enjoyed considerable media coverage. Parks' house now became a symbol, this time because it did not remain seated, so to speak. From *El Jahziraa* to *CNN*, the media talked about "America's shame" and reported on abandoned, forgotten communities in Detroit. It seems that the house had to be brought to Berlin for its story to be told. The artist says: "*The Rosa Parks house should be a national monument and not a demolition project*" and "*This house is happily here, I believe. Because it finds itself in a city that honors tolerance.*" Hm. Somehow a nice, even hopeful story. But is so much praise for the "*suburb of freedom*" justified and necessary?

At the end of 2017 the house returned to the USA, to be exhibited at the Rhode Island School of Design. This time, the *Berliner Zeitung* complained that Berlin had once again missed an opportunity – arguing that the house could have given the new *Humboldtforum* museum complex in the rebuilt city palace "*historical depth*". An interesting thought. In 2018 the house was offered for sale by New York auction house Guernsey as part of an auction titled *African American Historic & Cultural Treasures*, together with letters by Rosa Parks and Martin Luther King. The minimum bid was 1 million dollars; the auction house wrote that it hoped for some cultural institution to be interested in this historically important object. It didn't sell during the auction, but Guernsey reported negotiations had begun with an interested party.

[The *Haus der Statistik* (House of Statistics) 2019; the proposed name for the *Alexanderplatz, Allesandersplatz* ("It's all different"-Square), perfectly expresses the basic need of Berliners and Germans to be different. The future of the building complex is uncertain, from studios, integration house, residential buildings to the new Rathaus Mitte, everything is possible and probably also planned.]

What remains to be said ...

Berlin.

I admit, when I moved to West-Berlin a long, long time ago from one of the regions of the world known to locals as "provincial" (i.e. another German city), I was not exclusively enthusiastic. The pomp and splendor of the broad, often boastful streets seemed to echo imperial Germany's arrogant sides to me, and somehow I even managed to be doubtful of West-Berlin's aristocracy of alternative cool that was all the rage at the time, not least in Kreuzberg. I had certainly not discovered the "front city" idealistically at work on a future, free, unrestricted human society without power structures I had somehow imagined. In fact, blatant consumerism reigned supreme along the Ku'damm – during the day in the luxurious shops, at night on the street itself, which functioned as an analog escort site, with flashy female sex workers offering their perfect skin to whoever had the cash. But first impressions are often misleading, or perhaps one just gets used to everything, and then the Wall came down. In the 1990s Berlin somehow became more of what optimistic newcomers like me had dreamed of – unusual, new terrain with a feeling of anarchy to it, but more or less devoid of people insisting on the right of the strong or the rich (to be sure, bullies and moneyheads existed – but I believe they were simply not in on the fun, or the excitement), meaning everything seemed possible. Even the art establishment with its, hm, creative version of power structures and networks had not yet claimed the city; the arts scene was more a common way of life than something professionals could make a living of or slap a price tag on. But as said: first impressions are deceptive. At some point Berlin became a magnet for tourists, hipsters, marketing teams, professional artists and other such gentrifiers, as well as for all those who tired of high rental costs elsewhere. Did Berlin, whose mayor claimed it to be *"poor but sexy"* in those days and tried to recruit international, desirable new citizens with the battle cry *"Be Berlin!"*, after all its years of being a place on the less streamlined periphery of the West, start to transform into just another European big city – including the typical hike in rents and the usual social upheavals, during which all undesirables (non-rich people) would be gently forced out of the more coveted areas and structures? Or is it all just phoney, a work of fiction, a transient thing, in keeping with the assertion by art critic Karl Scheffler – not necessarily meant positively, made in 1910 and often quoted – that Berlin is *"damned to always become, but to never be"*?

Casting my mind back to my early days in West-Berlin, I remember a conversation in the *Kumpelnest*, back then the place to be for everyone who just didn't belong anywhere, with one of the "usual suspects" of the times. We talked, as one does, about this and that; the burden of Germany's past, the unloved heritage of our deeply suspicious ancestors, which practically everyone I knew wanted to escape from into a future that was, in a very positive sense, uncertain. We had left our native provincial backwaters and come to West-Berlin[92] – which we, with unfounded optimism, called a *"blank slate"* (we really thought of our lives, our culture, the road we were going to take as a new, unprecedented thing). A blank slate for us to fill in. West-Berlin was, in our young and simple minds, an *unwritten* place. It also did look a bit like it was rubbed clean the hard way, with its expansive zones of war-torn wasteland, the ragged *Niemandsland* (no-man's-land) opposite the *Kulturforum* (now widely known as Potsdamer Platz), the often run-down rather than renovated old buildings, the many inappropriate, awkward or ugly looking new buildings and the handful of almost utopian-seeming exceptions such as the *Philharmonie* and the *Haus der Kulturen der Welt*. This was somehow a foggy parallel world—one that, in winter, reeked of coal, in which people debated (or drank, flirted, dominoed etc.) the winter nights away in bars to avoid their freezing homes. Today Berlin is a prime example of a defined city, and those who decide to go out practically always experience whatever they pay for, alternative and cool as it might look and feel. You often come across tourist groups being given detailed lectures on what is so special about Berlin, what happened where back when, where there was an East and West, how important which graffiti and which clubs and places were and are, and how they should evaluate and understand all this. Along with some tips

---

[92] At the time, young men often came to West-Berlin to escape conscription; or the duty to become "men", in the stupidest sense.

as to where to go today to be cool, these wholesale describers of Berlin (or any other place) strive to "allow" or "enable" (in the horrible modern sense of the word) listeners to understand Berlin. Just as this text does. Well – hopefully not.

Berlin, it has to be said, is OK. Sometimes it is momentarily great in its here and now – and in this respect Berlin is very similar to everywhere else. For me, Berlin is special when tiny flickers of a non-elitist (which pretty much also means non-hipster – sorry) utopia are kindled. But Berlin is a big city, one that has always attracted people who had hopes for a better life, a decent livelihood, for a place where they could realize their dreams and ideas or would find people who would pay for their products – or simply for themselves. The industrialists and artists, the ladies of the night and the managers of others, the speculative landlords and brokers and the whatnots, all the usual motley crew that makes up our societies.

"Paris is a garden, Brussels is blooming, Antwerp is proliferating – but Berlin is constructed. The city wasn't born, it made itself."

(Wilhelm Hausenstein)

But it just may be that Berlin is indeed peculiar, different, a place of, often misplaced, hope. After all, it didn't get much of an inheritance – no Roman prehistory, no raw materials, no really, really big river as a natural trade route, no nearby sea port, no mountains or other impressive natural structures, no abundant sunshine; even its human assets had to be imported on repeated occasions. No wonder that Berlin, in its best moments, is a strange construct deformed by time that somehow, but never concretely, promises freedom. It can promise little else. But is it a false promise?

And of course, Berlin is always changing. As is the world. And you often wonder if those changes are for good, although you hardly ever dare to say such things out loud: the show must go on. There is, for example, the thing with affordable rents − calculated optimism (if you don't have an old lease), if you ask me. Still, even Berliners who often can't change flats anymore will say *"but it's cheaper than elsewhere"*. Sometimes there are moments when you have to pull yourself together not to laugh out loud.

From the dodgy laboratory of discussion and reinvention, which people like to locate here, the city has developed into a place celebrating the standard coexistence of groups and nationalities. And yes: there have always been some new Berliners with a tendency to tenderly look down on stereotyped Germans who have, for example, no natural rhythm, are less fun (present company always excluded), somehow bourgeois, or not really part of the modern world. Maybe. Even if it is tempting, German-born Berlin residents should not succumb to the (very German) tendency to feel like the unloved and underpaid operators of an amusement park. It is likely just an expression of the possibly and lamentably completely anti-utopian human nature, which feels more comfortable, more smug by dividing itself into existing, defining groups. And there are, luckily, plenty examples of deviant behavior in Berlin, too – of a shared hope for a non-stereotypical world, of a belief in individuality. Luckily.

There are often reports of experiences between Berliners who do or do not belong to ethnic minorities and/or visitors which can be classified as ... hostile. For Berlin is certainly not only the welcoming, cosmopolitan city which it bills itself as, and Germans with their disparate backgrounds are not always shining examples of tolerance and/or friction-free coexistence. Sometimes, it has to be said, Berlin seems a horrible place. Even those who have lived here for a long time, such as the author, often wonder if it wouldn't just make more sense to move to a nicer climate, to hopefully avoid the ever-increasing conflicts between successful and failed attempts at life, to avoid the blatant stupidity of right-wingers, and the very German and constant bickering (mostly about politics). Thus, at some point living in Berlin becomes one thing above all: the question of whether the promise of Berlin is still big enough, open enough, realistic enough to remain in the city. The answer must be delivered every day, every week anew.

One thing that makes Berlin so incredibly German for me is that it is, mostly, a place of longing, a place of wanting to be elsewhere, of locally implemented *wanderlust*. Berlin, in stark contrast to other capitals, does not (yet) seem to be a place that celebrates its "national brand" much. From the longing for the splendor of the French courts displayed by aristocrats who felt German was a language for the barbarians they had to take care of, made accessible in Sanssouci in Potsdam, to Berlin's classicism that tried to create an *"Athens on the Spree"*[93] culturally ruled by poets, artist and thinkers supported by fanpeople to the mansions somewhat resembling English palaces of the super-rich of the late 1800s and the wish of many immigrants to escape their culturally often less liberal places of origin (among them predominantly the German hinterland). Perhaps, perhaps Berlin was most "itself" in its both bourgeois and revolutionary tendencies between the founding of the *Reich* and WW I, and then, perhaps, perhaps, perhaps, a little in the Weimar period, nowadays mostly remembered in poptastically commercial ways as a place of drugs and sex and hard-but-heartful living, a time that was in fact marked by blatant poverty, often misguided approaches at remaking the society, and, of course, all the temptations and dangers of the *"Hure Babylon"*, as writer

[93] Or a Rome on the Spree; the term *Spree-Athen* was coined in the 18th century and alluded to the cultural achievements of Prussia; Schinkel belongs in the broader sense to the circle of "German-Romans" who drew inspiration from stays in Italy. But despite the "classical" look of his buildings, Schinkel in particular was always interested in modern techniques and implementation possibilities.

Alfred Döblin described the city. Or perhaps the city is now itself, as it is (again) in the process of shedding any home-grown culture – this time for the sake of a ruling class longing for international cultural recognition and relevance, which sees the common Berliner only as a paying, gladly enthusiastic claqueur or raw material for cultural experiments. Wait a minute. Is that true? Hm. Perhaps, and this would be the most beautiful, dangerous, optimistic and also standard reading, Berlin is not yet Berlin; or will never be. Is that why the ads scream: "*Be Berlin?*"

Go ahead: be Berlin if you want to, even if it sounds a bit like a sellout. The *defined* city is always also the *advertised* city. If you trust the official advertising posters, Berliners live out their sexuality unabashedly in tolerant, pretty open relationships; they're friendly, cosmopolitan, and obviously not plagued by existential fears (cheap rent). Hm. Sounds like a blueprint for the taxpayers the city has on its Xmas list. The reality is, as usual, more difficult. But of course they exist, these ultra-satisfied Be-Berliners. Sometime ago I heard an interview on the radio with a woman living in Berlin who said that, after work, she likes to go to one of the clubs on the Spree, sit down with a drink in the sunset, and enjoy "this city". Nice. Still, something inside me started to sit uneasily. But since I like to stay a little, hm, faithful to my adopted city, I thought of other quotes describing Berlin. The Spaniard Javier Marias said at some point that the reason for life being so easy-going in Berlin and Madrid was that people didn't think too much of their cities.[94] An interesting point. And in his *Berliner Kindheit* (Berlin Childhood), Walter Benjamin wrote *"then, the city was as absorbed in itself, just like a sack heavy with me and my happiness"*. The quote immediately reconciled me with my surroundings, and I sat down by the Spree with a drink to stare at the sunset.

[94] I am told that practically all inhabitants of all cities (the example provided to me was Londoners) like to complain about their cities – amongst themselves. Visitors, though, should normally refrain from doing so. Any criticism will be met with abundant praise for the city or culture in question.

My thanks

Abundant, comprehensive and always incomplete thanks to Sandra M., who was always ready to supply advice, support and criticism, and to Kassi W. and Susann L. To Francis L. for his always kind and helpful linguistic suggestions and insights. To the team at the Reisebuch-Verlag. And of course to all the peace-loving inhabitants of and visitors to Berlin, and the always strange and beautiful German language. With that in mind:

West-Berlin and East Berlin. Really?

Yeah, that seems weird. But we had some discussions that eventually led to the spelling in this text, which, at first glance, may seem ill-considered. In my memory, and that of most West Germans I spoke to about the matter, "West-Berlin" was the usual writing (in German). The East Berlin media typically wrote "Westberlin" (there was no East Berlin, only "Berlin, Capital of the GDR"). The hyphen, officially raised to the rank of "hyphen of freedom" in a *Tagesspiegel* article from 2013, is supposed to have pointed out, in a feely-grammarly way, that the division of the city was believed to be temporary. Hm. A side note: not all West-Berliners were looking for reunification; some trusted the *Kapitalistniks* (West) no more than the *Apparatchiks* (East) and believed in something more closely located in the philosophical-political middle ground (or in cosy alternative niches with social security supplied by tax-paying *Normalos*, as some contended with corrosive grins), or even wished for a completely new state instead of a unified Germany: a tainted culture that had assumed the guilt of its various predecessors and, to some minds, had lacked the courage for a real revolution and a complete break with its past.

In this sense, one could then speak of a "hyphen of possibilities" or "hyphen of utopia". "Ber-lin" might be a good name for a future utopian city. As we see, the local language usage became one of the many

Sources

for the stories presented here. But of course: the most important source for the material of these ramblings is the general information store called the Internet, especially its various Wikipedia variants. References to stories such as those collected here can, however often be found on the streets; on commemorative plaques; in conversations with friends and acquaintances; in literature; in newspapers. In a hyphen. In life. And in the

Bibliography

— Here are some books on the subject at hand; some I consulted, others are mere recommendations. Some are non-fiction books, others comprise literature of various types. One or two might be familiar to most readers. I found them all stimulating and worth the time.

Benjamin, Walter: Berlin Childhood circa 1900 (1950, posthumous; various translations)

Berndorff, L. & Friedrich, T. (Hrsg.): 1000 Tage, die die Welt bewegten (2008)

Cullen, Michael S.: The Reichstag (1999)

Döblin, Alfred: Berlin Alexanderplatz (1929; various translations)

Harris, Robert: Fatherland (1992)

Heisenberg, Werner: Quantentheorie und Philosophie

Hermann, Georg: Jettchen Gebert (1906)

Isherwood, Christopher: Goodbye to Berlin (1939)

Mailänder, Uli & Zander, Ulrich: Das kleine Westberlin-Lexikon (2003)

Mende, H.-J. & Wernicke, K. (Hrsg.): Berlin Mitte – Das Lexikon (2001)

Richie, Alexandra: Faust's Metropolis: A History of Berlin (1998)

Scheffler, Karl: Berlin – Ein Stadtschicksal (1910)

Schuhmann, Axel: Berliner Presse und Französische Revolution (2001)

Skármeta, Antonio: No pasó nada (1978)

Siedler, Wolf Jobst: Abschied von Preußen (1998)

Zuse, Konrad: The Computer – My Life (1969; various translations)

Index

Weitere Titel von Travis Elling im *Reisebuch Verlag* Reisebuch Verlag

Andalusien *anders* entdecken

Reisen in Spaniens Süden durch
Vergangenheit und Gegenwart

ISBN 978-3-947334-35-3

Deutschsprachige Ausgabe von
Explore Berlin

ISBN 978-3-947334-36-0

Diese und weitere spannende Reisebücher unter
www.reisebuchverlag.de!